Centerport Fire Department
1898 - 1998

A reflection on how Centerport has changed and grown over the past 100 years

Published by The Centerport Fire Department, Centerport, N.Y.

Printed by: Printer Colombiana S.A.
Printed in Colombia.

ISBN# 0-9670483-0-3

Library of Congress Catalog Number: 99-60975

Dedication

In this our centennial year, we, the members of the Centerport Fire Department, dedicate this book to all the men and women who have ever served in the Centerport Fire Department and the Citizens, whose support has enabled us to serve them.

We give our thanks to all of the men and women who serve as firefighters and rescue personnel regardless of the time or day, and to their families who have sacrificed, so that they can serve the community. The support of the community; the countless cards, letters, and donations has allowed Centerport to remain one of the best and safest communities.

We appreciate the assistance of the Ladies' Auxiliary, whose efforts strengthen the members of the Fire Department.

We give thanks to all our sponsors, without you there would be no book. We also acknowledge all the members of the 100th Book Committee for their countless hours of research and to the historians who had the foresight to preserve our past so that we can reflect back.

Centerport F.D.
100 years of dedicated service

CELEBRATING OUR CENTENNIAL

Chiefs of the Centerport Fire Department

1898	JAMES HOWARD
1899-1902	HENRY DENTON
1903-1904	FRANKLIN MORRIS
1905	THEODORE SAMMIS
1906-1910 &	
1912-1914	JOHN BUNCE
1911	FREDERICK COTRELL
1915-1920	GEORGE BUNCE
1921-1926	WALTER ROWLAND
1927, 1929-1931	THOMAS UTTER
1928	EDWARD MILLER
1932, 1937 &	
1945-1946	BYRON NICHOLS
1932-1934	HAROLD WITTING
1935	HAROLD POPLEES
1936	ANTON POLACEK JR.
1938-1944	ERHARDT GRAULICH
1947-1948	GEORGE SIMPSON
1949-1951	JOSEPH JARET
1952-1953	WILLIAM WAMP
1954-1955	ROBERT GANGLOFF
1956-1957	RICHARD REYNOLDS
1958-1959	EARL SAMMIS
1960	WILLIAM SWAN JR.
1961-1962	WILLIAM KELSEY
1963	HARRY BURR
1964-1965	JOHN KEARNEY
1966-1967	KENNETH SWAN
1968-1969	KENNETH KLERK
1970-1971	DOUGLAS DAVIDSON
1972-1973	DONALD MILLER
1974-1975	EDWIN SEIM
1976-1977	LOUIS RISPOLI
1978	WILLIAM BOHATY
1979, 1981	WILLAM WAMP JR.
1980	LOUIS SCARDUZIO
1982-1983	PATRICK FALLON
1984-1985	JAMES FEELEY
1986-1987	GEORGE PRIBYL
1988-1989	PAUL STEVENSON
1990-1991	ANDREW MARK
1992-1993	GUS ZEIS
1994-1995	PETER GUNTHER
1996-1997	PAUL HEGLUND
1998 -	ROBERT SIMPSON

Robert Simpson
Chief of the Department

It has been with great pride and honor to be Chief of the Centerport Department during its 100th year anniversary. In addition to celebrating 100 years of dedicated service, we had two past chiefs, Ken Klerk and Earl Sammis, celebrate 50 years of service to the Fire Department.

After 100 years of service to the community, the true principal of a volunteer firefighter has not changed. Time, commitment, and continuous training are the biggest challenges the members face on a daily basis. As technology progresses so must the Centerport Fire Department.

I hope we can continue to serve the community with the same professionalism and dedication for the next 100 years, for we are the unpaid professional firefighters that I can proudly say are the members of the Centerport Fire Department.

James Feeley
1st Assistant Chief

As I look back on my time in the Centerport Fire Department our newly restored 1944 Mack fire truck was the first line fire apparatus for the fire department in the mid 1960's. We saw a need for upgrading our rescue capabilities, and in the 1970's acquired a second ambulance and instituted Advanced Life capabilities on both ambulances. Through the 80's we realized the need for surface and scuba rescue, and the department developed a Water Rescue Team which was cutting edge at the time. The department also saw the need and purchased a piece of aerial fire apparatus to provide the latest fire protection to its residents.

The volunteer members of the fire department make all this possible. Over the last 30+ years the volunteer has been asked over and over to increase their time for training to a point where in our 100th year a volunteer is putting in nearly 5 times the amount of training they did in the 60's. I am very proud of all our members not only today but in the past, for without their continued time and training, this volunteer service would not have realized a 100th anniversary.

Kevin Dearie
2nd Assistant Chief

In Centerport Fire Department's centennial year, our predecessors, whose photographs grace our walls, would be both astonished and proud of our evolution since 1898.

It is our privilege to follow in the footsteps of those dedicated volunteers who came before us. By working together for the safety and betterment of the community in which we live, and which we serve, we strive to leave Centerport and our Department as positive monuments to our service and dedication, as did those before us.

As 2nd Assistant Chief, I begin the path followed by the past chiefs of our department. I am honored to work and serve with all the dedicated men and women of this department.

In my nearly 16 years as a member of this department I have learned that we make a difference, and we should be proud of that!

I have watched our department go through many changes over the years, and I look forward to meeting the challenges that are facing us in the future.

Presidents of The Centerport Fire Department

1934	DR. JOHN REB
1935	HENRY HOWE
1936-37	THOMAS SAUNDERS
1938-44	JOSEPH R. MORAN
1945-48	ALFRED HARRIS
1949-51	HARRY PEARSALL
1952-53	ROBERT J. BOHATY
1954-55	ROBERT SPENCE
1956-57	ANTHONY PRIORE
1958-59	OTTO HEINICKE
1960-61	BART HEANEY
1962-63	JAMES ARMSTRONG
1964-65	LEROY JARET
1966-67	WILLIAM SWAN JR.
1968	ROBERT SAMEK
1969-70	J. GREG SULLIVAN
1971-72	KEVIN GALLAGHER
1973	JEROME KUBICKI
1974-75	PATRICK SANTOMAURO
1976-77	GEORGE TISCHNER
1978	EDWARD HALLENBACK
1979	EDWIN R. SEIM
1980-81	JAMES M. COX
1982-83	WALTER NASS
1984-85	SAMUEL JONES
1986-87	JAMES REILLY
1988	DAVE MC GOVERN
1989-90	TOM P. FEELEY
1991-92	PATRICIA BRUCE
1993-94	JAMES O'DONNELL
1995-96	CLIFFORD R. RAYNOR
1997-98	WILLIAM PENNY

William E. Penny
President of the Department

To be President during our 100th Anniversary has been an honor for me. Those before me have laid the foundation and allowed us to make the first 100 years possible. The real task will be to continue and grow for the next 100 years. I would like to thank the Board of Directors, the 100th Anniversary Committee, and the Chiefs for a job well done.

Mary "Gallagher" Ryan
1st Vice-President

Being part of the Board of Directors during our 100th Anniversary has been both challenging and fulfilling. Part of the 1st Vice Presidents job is running our annual fund drive. This task involves about 3000 households in the Centerport Fire District receiving our donation request, which supports the activities of the Department. Volunteering for the Centerport Fire Department for almost 15 years and being a junior firefighter for 4 years has influenced my life tremendously; it has given me direction and makes me proud to volunteer for such a worthy cause. I thank the community for their support and would encourage you to join our department.

Jack W. Geffken, D.O.
2nd Vice-President

A lot has changed since I first joined the Department back in 1981. The cost of living has soared and this has put a strain on volunteerism. Being there and making a difference is worth the time I donate. I encourage others to volunteer otherwise one day the things we take for granted may be gone.

As Chairman of the 100th Book Committee I would like to thank my wife, Debbie, and my sons, Ryan & Shawn, for the countless evenings I spent on the computer to make this book happen.

A Fireman's Prayer

When I am called to duty, god, whenever flames may rage;
Give me strength to save some life, whatever be its age.

Help me embrace a little child before it is too late
Or save an older person from the horror of that fate.

Enable me to be alert and hear the weakest shout,
And quickly and efficiently to put the fire out.

I want to fill my calling and to give the best in me,
To guard my every neighbor and protect his property.

And if, according to my fate, I am to lose my life;
Please bless with your protecting hand my children and my wife.

Centerport

Originally settled in the late 1600's it was known as Stoney Brook and was inhabited by the Matinecock Indians. By 1700 its name had changed to Little Cow Harbor. The proximity to the water led to the shipbuilding and milling industry, a paper mill was built in the 1600's on the northwest corner of Route 25A and Centershore road where it remained in operation until its dam burst destroying it. This mill was rebuilt and burned in 1846 was rebuilt again in 1850 and converted to grain processing in 1881. In 1774 the Titus mill was built by damming off the harbor. Centerport in the past was a deep water harbor berthing three schooners. These ships would take grain to the mill and transport the flour it made to many places including New York City. The Titus mill was rehabilitated in 1849 where it ran strong until it's demolition in 1915, some timbers remain on display at the Vanderbilt museum and the grinding stone can be seen on display in Huntington's Village Green. The end of the Little Neck area was owned by the Sills family where they mined sand and clay for their business, the Northport Fire Sand & Clay Company, in the late 1700's. The Sills house is now the Centerport Beach Senior Citizens building. 1836 saw the first schoolhouse for Centerport which had only 1 room. In 1831 Centerport (Little Cow Harbor) built its first post office . The post office moved several times but has always been in the Centershore Road area. In 1836 Little Cow Harbor became Centreport which was changed to Centerport in 1895 to make the name sound more American. The railroad could not be constructed in Centerport because of its topography so it went into Greenlawn instead, but interestingly it was called the Centerport Station until 1870. Centerport was a retreat for many and tourism, boarding houses and restaurants thrived until the early 1900's when tourism began to fade. The Chalmer's house was the largest among the boarding houses and was located on the property now known as Camp Alvernia. The Chalmer's house charged $1.50 a day or $8 week to stay and was purchased by the Franciscan Brothers in 1888 and turned into, what is currently, the oldest catholic camp in the United States.

A drawing of Centerport in 1881 by artist Ed Lange

ADASZEWSKI, EDWARD	FLOOD, DANIEL	MOSELEY, ROBERT
ADASZEWSKI, PHILIP	FOISSET, AUGUST	MURRAY, CHRISTOPHER
AHLSEN, ROY	FOX, JOSEPH	NAPLES, NORMAN
AHLSEN, WAYNE	FRERES, EDWARD	NATIELLO, DONATO
ANCEWICZ, EDWARD	GARDINER, FREDERICK	NIEMCZYK, JEROME
ANCEWICZ, GREGORY	GARILLI, JOHN	NIEMCZYK, JEROME JR.
ANCEWICZ, LAWRENCE	GIBBS, PETER	NUNES, JEFFERY
ANCEWICZ, MARK	GRASLEY, ROBERT	NUNES, MANUEL
ANDERSON, HAROLD	GRUEBEL, RONALD	O'LEARY, WILLIAM
ARDITO, FRANK	GUNSEL, SCOTT	O'SULLIVAN, JOHN
BARBERA, ANTHONY	HAGEMANN, ERIC	PELKOFSKY, RONALD
BAROSS, JOHN	HARDESTY, RICHARD	PERKOWSKI, FELIX
BAUDO, DANIEL	HARTNETT, PAUL	PERKOWSKI, THEODORE
BEIGELBECK, ANTHONY	HARTNETT, THOMAS	POKORNY, JOHN
BIANCO, FRANCIS	HENRIKSON, JOHN	RABE, WALTER
BIANCO, KRISTEN	HENRIKSON, KENNETH	RAITI, STEPHEN
BIVONA, BARNEY	HENRIKSON, KENNETH JR	REINERT, STEPHEN
BIVONA, CHARLES	HERTZEL, SPENCER	RINKER, GALE
BIVONA, ROBERT	HOLIK, RONALD	SADOWSKI, STANLEY
BOROWY, WILLIAM	HOUSTON, SEAN	SAUSA, JACK
BRUSH, GILBERT	IRVING, EDWARD	SAUSA, JOHN
BUNYAN, PAUL	IRVING, JOHN	SCOTT, JOHN
BURKE, KEVIN	IRVING, WILLIAM	SEALS, NICHOLAS
BURKE, TIMOTHY	JESBERGER, LAWRENCE	SENATORE, ROBERT
BYERS, BRUCE	JOHNSON, EDWARD	SHAW, JOHN
CAPUTO, DANIEL	JORGENSON, PETER	SIMONSON, RUSSEL
CAPUTO, DAVID	JOSEPH, LEE	SMITH, GORDON
CEGLIA, EDWARD	KELLY, FRANCIS	SMITH, KELLY
CLEMENT, KEITH	KRATZ, OTTO	STATTON, ALBERT
COFFEY, KYLE	KUHLMANN, ERIC	STOCKMAN, BRUCE
CORRIGAN, THOMAS	KUHLMANN, WILLIAM	STUBING, HENRY
CORWIN, MICHAEL	LEMP, THOMAS	TAMBORSKI, GARY
COSTELLO, JOSEPH	LEPERA, FRANK	TAVERNESE, JOESPH
CRAYNE, JAMES	LEWIS, DONALD	TEWKSBURY, DOUGLAS
CREAMER, THOMAS	MARKHAM, KEVIN	TILDEN, BRUCE
DALRYMPLE, SCOTT	MAZZONE, LARRY	TILDEN, HERBERT
DALY, KEVIN	MCALPIN, CONRAD	TILDEN, LEE
DEMAREST, SCOTT	MCDONALD, ROBERT	TROTTMAN, THOMAS
DEMAYO, FRANCIS	MCKEE, CLIFFORD	VERRILLI, ALBERT
DEMPSEY, CHRISTOPHER	MCKENNA, JOHN	VILLA, CHARLES
DERISO, FRANK	MCLAUGHLIN, KYLE	VOIGHT, HENRY
DERISO, FRANK M	MCWILLIAMS, TIMOTHY	WACHTIN, ALAN
DORN, MICHAEL	MCWILLIAMS, WALTER	WAGENHAUSER, FREDRICK
DZIENIUS, FRANK	MELCHIOR, CLIFFORD	WAGENHAUSER, KURT
FAY, KEVIN	MICHALOWSKI, ANTHONY	WARYOLD, SCOTT
FELLMETH, CHARLES	MILLER, PETER	WEISS, HANS
FELLMETH, STEVEN	MILTNER, RICHARD	WEISS, JOHN
FERGUSON, DAVID	MISILEWICH, DAVID	WEYERMULLER, GERHARD
FITZSIMMONS, DAVID	MISKISKY, STEVEN	WHEELER, EDWARD
	MODELEWSKI, EDWARD	WIECK, WILLIAM
	MODZELEWSKI, JOHN	WILLIAMS, HARRY JR.
	MORAN, GREGORY	WOODHOUSE, ROBERT
	MORAN, LEON	ZEIS, MICHAEL
	MORE, ALFRED	

CONGRATULATIONS
ON YOUR 100TH ANNIVERSARY
FROM ALL THE MEN AND WOMEN
OF THE
GREENLAWN FIRE DEPARTMENT

Compliments of

The officers and men of:

The Northport Fire Department

Compliments of

The officers and men of:

The East Northport Fire
Department

1880 - Benham's General Store & Post Office -Located on Centershore Road across from the current P.O.

1882 - Centerport's 2nd school. It was located on Park Circle just East of the Firehouse
Photo on the right courtesy of the Huntington Historical Society

1884 - MillDam Bridge - The Eastern half was only a catwalk

1898 - The Original Firehouse - located just West of the current Firehouse

In 1898, after experiencing the harsh destruction of area property by several fires, residents of "Centreport" recognized the need for an organized fire department. In response to this need, the community came together at a meeting at the local schoolhouse on September 7, to discuss plans for its creation. On September 10, $95.20 was allocated for the construction of a truck house and sixteen days later John Robinson, Edward D. Mott and Jonas A. Titus were elected as trustees for terms of three years, two years and one year respectively. On October 1, 1898, the first Department By-laws were voted on and accepted by the members. On November 23, 1898, Articles of Incorporation were obtained establishing the Centerport Fire Department. The charter members of the Centerport Fire Department were :

John N. Benham	Jesse S. Bunce	C. Franklin Bunce
John S. Bunce	George E. Doty	Charles Higbie Jr.
James Howard	Joshua Ketcham	Theo B. Sammis
Edward P. Soper	David H. Smith	John N.R. Smith
Frank H. Suydam	Jonas A. Titus	William H. Van Nostrand

The building committee obtained lumber from Newton Creek and after much hard work and determination, the original firehouse was completed on December 3, 1898, less than three months from the first meeting. The Department was self-supporting and relied on its member dues of $.25 per month to pay expenses. At the time, no fire hydrants existed in the area and there was no Department uniform.

On December 3, 1898 the first meeting was held and officers were elected. James H. Howard was Chief, David H. Smith the Foreman, and Frank H. Suydam the Assistant Foreman. John N.R. Smith was elected Treasurer, and Fred Chalmers the Secretary. On December 15, 1898 the Fire Department hosted a supper for the residents of Centerport. Apparently the Chief attended this function in a somewhat "altered" condition. Two days later the Foreman requested an apology from the Chief for his inappropriate behavior at the supper. The Chief refused and tendered his resignation, which was accepted. His total term of service was two weeks long!

The second Chief of the Centerport Fire Department was Henry H. Denton, whose tenure lasted from September 2, 1898 to September 5, 1903, which was considerably longer than the term of his predecessor. On March 3, 1899, it was decided that a Fireman's Fair would be held the second week of every August behind the Firehouse. You will read more about this event later on. During the course of 1899, it was decided that not more than $600.00 was to be put toward the purchase of new fire apparatus and that blue uniforms were to be worn for all practice drills and at quarterly meetings.

Thanks to the Long Island Railroad, the Centerport Fire Department was equipped with a metal railroad tire that, when struck, alerted members of alarms. An open pavilion was erected in the rear of the Firehouse complete with a boardwalk on the roof and a frame of

Chief James Howard 1898

Chief Henry Denton 1899-1902

locust posts, which held the tire iron hoop.
Members were notified of alarms by way of
the iron hoop which, when struck with a long
handled maul, rang out clearly. The men
would race to the firehouse and the first
horses there would be hooked up to pull the
fire carts.

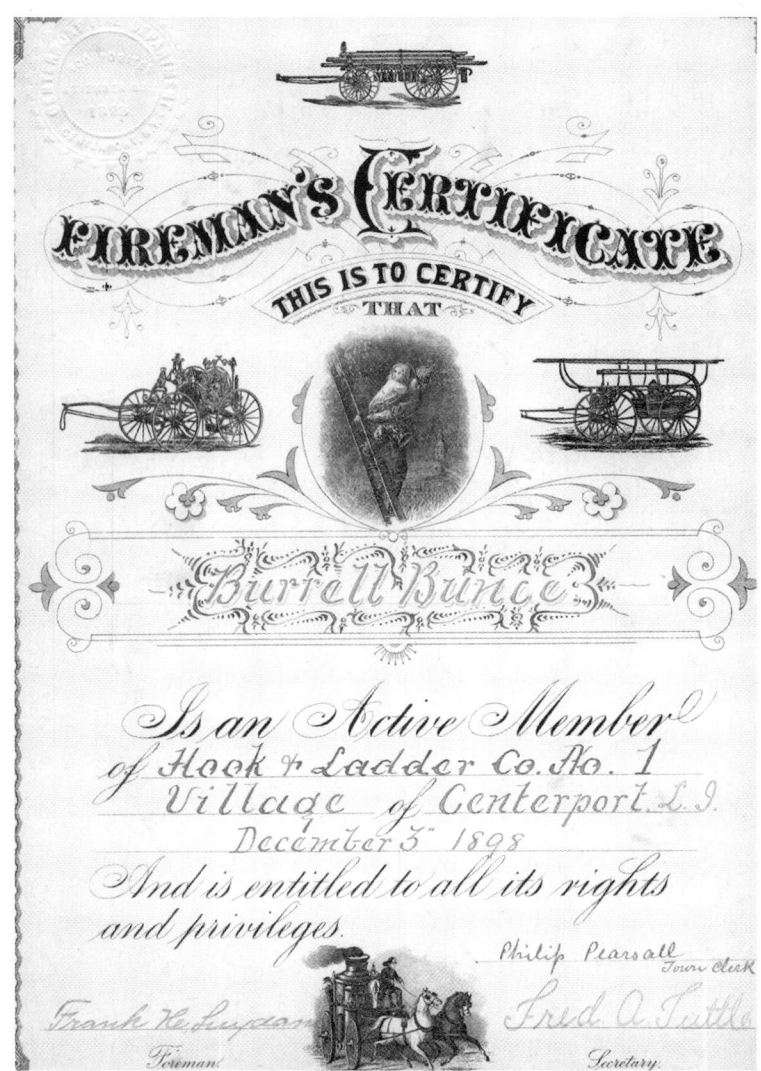

An original Certificate of Membership

The first members responding to an alarm would
hook their horses up to haul the equipment

The first official annual meeting occurred on
September 2, 1899 at which time it was decided that
fireman Bunce was to serve as Department janitor
and collect a salary of $2.00 per month. This arrange-
ment lasted all of two months when, on November 4,
1899, Mr. Bunce turned in his resignation.
Centerport's first firehouse was wired and electrified
during the course of this year, costing the
Department a total of $14.50. This bill was paid in
full from the Department treasury, which had a
grand balance of $244.70!

1900 marked the year that a formal road was to be
constructed across the Mill Dam which had never
been completed. The highway commissioners
entertained several bids from contractors ranging
from Brooklyn to Patchogue. Ultimately, the contract
was awarded to George W. Brush of Northport.

1900 - Wards Inn on Centershore Road - next to the current Country Lake Adult Home
Photo courtesy of Susan Curran

Though he did not present the lowest bid at $3,198.00, Mr. Brush was granted the job because the commissioners believed that the contract should be given to a Town of Huntington resident. The road was completed on July 27, 1900.

During the course of 1900 the Centerport Fire Department conducted their first quarterly meeting, which included an inspection of uniforms. In addition, a new set of by-laws was adopted and it was agreed that a picture be taken of the entire company with the Department's truck. On July 7, 1900 it was decided that the Town of Huntington had to pay $20.00 for damages incurred to the fire truck due to improper care and maintenance of town roads. Also during this period, the first American flag used by the Centerport Fire Department was donated by Mr. A. Gilderstone of Halesite and was proudly displayed in the truckhouse.

1902 began with a frigid and wintry jolt. On February 20, 1902 a severe snowstorm crippled the area. Chief Denton ordered the alarm to be sounded for the purpose of getting manpower to help clear the roadways, but only four members were able to respond! As the year progressed, a proposal was made by New York and New Jersey telephone to install a fire alarm system for the members. The cost was to be $350.00. The proposal was tabled indefinitely due to lack of funding. On August 2, 1902, a committee was appointed to inspect a hand engine available for purchase. In addition, a motion was made that an Engine and Hose Company be formed and respectively called Company #2 and Hose Company #3.

At the forth Annual Meeting, held on September 6, 1902, it was agreed that the hand engine in question was found to be in fairly good condition and should be purchased for $149.27. The freight cost on the engine was $6.20. Officers were also elected for the ensuing year. H. Denton was elected Chief. B.F. Morris was elected Foreman for Company #1 with W. Mott his Assistant. Company #2 Foreman was Walter Rowland with W. Whiteman as Assistant and for Company #3, Thomas Stone was elected Foreman and Milton Rowland was elected his Assistant. The Secretary was J. Bunce, the Assistant Secretary, Frank H. Suydam and the Treasurer was J. Smith. On December 6, 1902 the Department purchased hose carts from Huntington Fire Department.

1903 was the year that the Ford Motor Company became incorporated and the Model A Runabout

Chief Franklin Morris
1903-1904

was sold. Locally, a Vaudeville team regularly used the west side of the Methodist Church for practice and it was rumored that they stayed at the old Echo estate (where the current catholic church stands). On March 6, 1903 a Director's meeting was called and an application which had been submitted by James Bunce was reviewed. Mr. Bunce requested permission to install a Barber's chair in the truckhouse. The motion was granted that evening and Mr. Bunce announced that he would shave everyone that night free of charge. Four months later, a pool table was purchased for $25.00 for the member's amusement. 1903 also marked the year that the Department participated in Huntington's 4th of July Parade. The men arrived on one large float dressed as Indians, with some members in a cannon and one member on a pony. On September 5, 1903 Chief Denton's resignation was accepted with regrets. Elections were held and B.F. Morris became Chief. W. Mott became Foreman of Company #1 with W. Rowland, Foreman of Company #2, and W. Whiteman, Foreman of Company #3.   T.B. Sammis was elected as Secretary and the Treasurer was J.A. Whaler. On October 3, 1903 a committee was formed to map out the boundaries of the fire protection area so that taxes would be able to be collected. In anticipation of these taxes, monthly dues were reduced from $.25 to $.10.

1904 marked the year that William K. Vanderbilt sponsored the first "Vanderbilt Cup Race for Motor Cars". This race took place on October 8 and traversed 220 miles of Long Island roadways starting in Westbury. Many came to view this spectacular event. Centerport Fire Department responded to several alarms in 1904 including a boat fire on the Schooner "J.B. Bowers". The fire occurred in Centerport Harbor and the schooner, which was owned by Thomas Bunce, sustained

The new addition

$300.00 worth of damage in the blaze. The men also responded to a working fire at The Robin's Nest Hotel on January 4, 1904, which incurred $150.00 worth of damage. In 1904, the members built an addition onto the already existing firehouse. This addition was initially sublet to Mr. Bunce who used it as a location for his barbershop. Years later, as the Department acquired more equipment, it became necessary for Mr. Bunce to vacate the premises. The addition was ultimately used as a truck bay.

 Several noteworthy, and profitable, events occurred in 1904. A 4th of July Ball was held complete with a fireworks display, which cost a mere $18.00. The Centerport Fireman's Fair ran successfully from August 16 to August 18 and the Firehouse was also rented out for $5.00 to Arthur Robinson for a wedding.

Chief Theodore Sammis 1905

In 1905, the world was introduced to Einstein's Theory of Relativity, the jukebox and the Yellow Pages! Locally, a group of concerned citizens organized the "Centerport Improvement Society" and donated $15,000.00 of their own money to insure the beautification of Centerport. With these funds, shrubs were planted and roadways were maintained. These projects were in addition to the services provided by the Town of Huntington. In 1905, proprietor Archie Hall owned and operated Doty's Hotel that was located in what is now Tung Ting's parking lot. This establishment was demolished in 1906 and was rebuilt across the street and renamed Hall's Hotel. The hotel was eventually sold and became Geide's Inn. Fire Department activities included the purchase of a 1000-pound bell and the formation of Companies known as Engine Company #1 and Hose Company #1.

In 1906, William K. Vanderbilt created the Long Island Motor Parkway Corporation with John Jacob Astor, Henry Ford, August Heckscher and August Belmont. These men constructed private roadways for the sole purpose of racing their vehicles. J. Bunce was Chief of the Centerport Fire Department and the purchase of a new foghorn for alarms was the highlight of the year. The foghorn, which was hand activated, is currently on display in our museum.

The "Centerport Improvement Society" subsidized the paving of a road from the Greenlawn Railroad Station to Centerport in 1907. This was done due to the Town of Huntington's refusal to pay for this project. In 1907, the Department consisted of 32 members. Headquarters was valued at $2000.00 and the equipment, valued at $1500.00, included a Hook and Ladder truck, a used hand engine, which earned the nickname "The Red Elephant", a hose cart, a Forest Fire Wagon, four

1904 - Chalmers House - located on Centerport Harbor where Camp Alvernia is now

Chief James Bunce
1906-1910 1912-1914

Chemical fire extinguishers, and 600 feet of hose. At a February meeting in 1907 a motion was made to purchase a large kettle for the purpose of making chowder. For reasons known only to them, the men decided that only male clams were to be used! The cost of the kettle was $3.25.

In 1908 the Centerport Fire Department had 30 active members, Mr. Bunce still served as Chief and the monthly dues were again $.25 per meeting due to the fact that taxes had yet to be collected. The Department's total value was determined to be $3,796.50, which included a Hook and Ladder Truck, valued at $600.00, an Engine, valued at $300.00, and a Hose Cart valued at $145.00. In 1908, it was decided that a "Waterman's Fountain Pen" was to be purchased for the Secretary at a cost of $4.25 and that $1.20 was to be paid to the Blacksmith, John Atkins, for work on Engine #1.

William K Vanderbilt

Halls Hotel - on the Corner of 25A & Centershore Roads

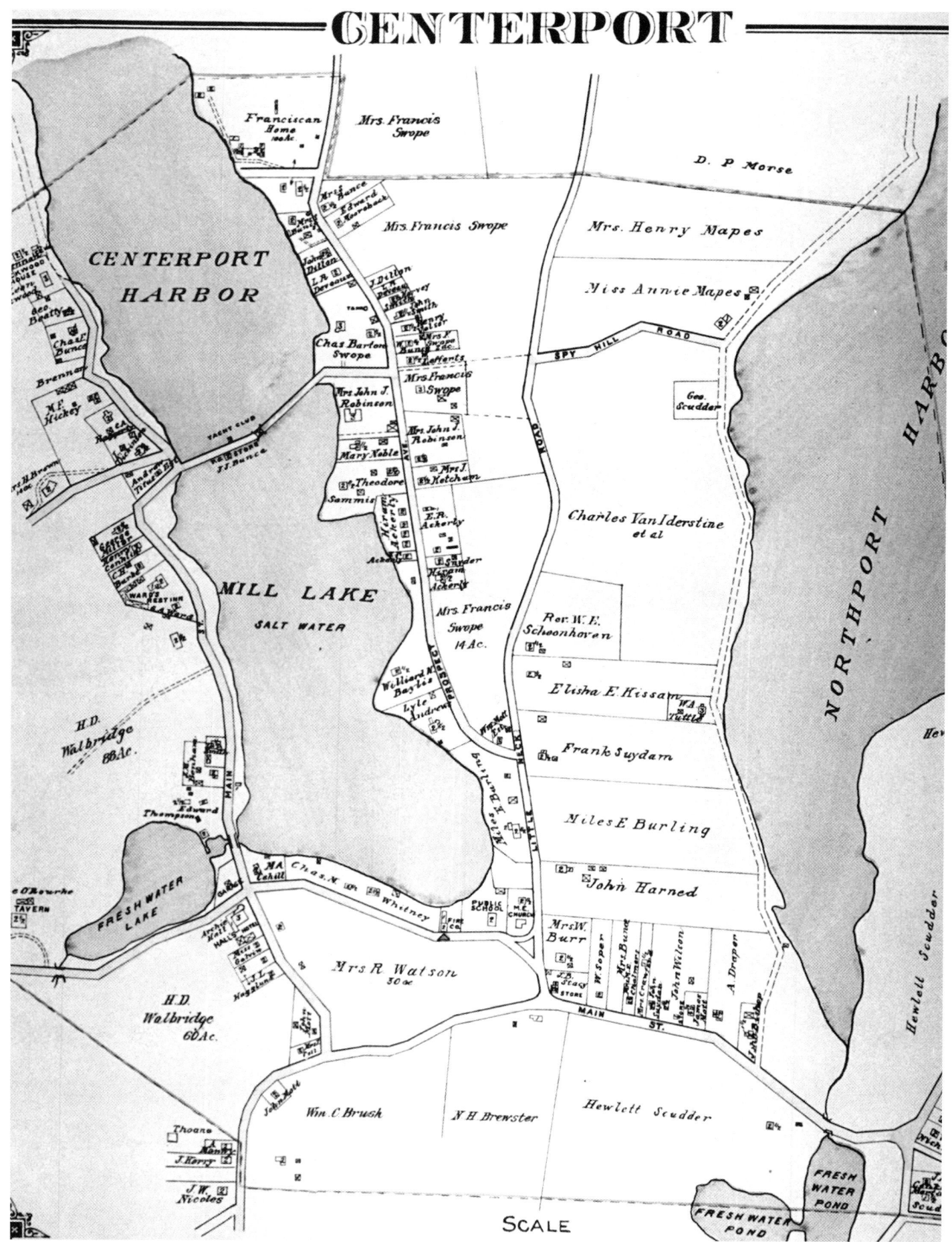

CENTERPORT

Centerport 1910 - notice the names of the roads and the dirt road that ran along Northport Harbor
Map courtesy of: Jack Geffken

The Old Mill on Centerport Harbor
Photo courtesy of: Jack Geffken

1909 was a rather quiet year for the Department. While J. Bunce remained as Chief, a decision was made in December to move the "outhouse" from Northport Road to the Firehouse. There was no charge for this service! In April, it was decided that the Centerport Fire Department would not attend the Queensboro Bridge opening on June 12.

In the year 1910, Centerport welcomed new resident William K. Vanderbilt II to the community. Mr. Vanderbilt moved into Eagle's Nest, now known as the Vanderbilt Museum. He became an active member of the Centerport Fire Department and served until 1944 when, at the age of 66, he retired. He is also remembered as having donated the Department's first ambulance, which you will read more about later. Within the Department, Chief Bunce mandated that members who neglected to wear their uniforms at the quarterly meetings be fined $.50. Also in 1910, a motion was made and carried to advertise the sale of the old engine and begin looking for a new one. In addition, the Department requested a book from New York State on mandated fire laws.

Incoming Chief, Fred Cotrell began his service on September 2, 1911 and during his term, several decisions were made to alter and improve the existing Firehouse. These improvements included the addition of railings on the side steps, an added 10 feet to the pavilion and the installation of girders in the main building. Centerport Fire Department also donated funds to the Fireman's Home in Hudson and agreed not to charge an admission fee to their annual summer fair.

Centerport Lake Overflow (25A/Centershore Rd)
Photo courtesy of: Jack Geffken

Chief Frederick Cortell 1911

John S. Bunce was elected Chief in 1912, which was the year that mail was first delivered by airplane. A new truck was purchased and anyone who donated money toward the purchase was considered an "honorary" member of the Department. In 1912, a motion was made and carried that all firemen were to attend church services in full uniform. Ultimately, the cost of these uniforms would be reimbursed to the member after two years of dedicated service.

1913 was another relatively quiet time for the Department. During the year, it was voted on and approved that the new truck to be purchased would be red and a mechanical engineer would be appointed to operate the new vehicle. It was also decided that gold buttons were to be given to all retiring Chiefs. Much to the delight of the Centerport community, the annual Fireman's Fair was held once again during the "dog days" of August and a great time was had by all.

Vanderbilt's original mansion and the eagles originally from Grand Central Station
Photo courtesy of The Vanderbilt Museum

Centerport F.D. - Circa 1910

The year was 1914, John S. Bunce remained as Chief and Thomas Utter was sworn in as a new member of the Department. Several improvements were made to the Firehouse during this time including telephone service, the addition of a screaming alarm, and the purchase of bunting for decoration. The men also felt it necessary to insure the fire truck. Also around this time, a tower was donated by August Heckscher of Huntington which the men reassembled on the east end of the Firehouse. The foghorn was then installed on top of the tower. In 1914, the Centerport Fire Department participated in the New York State Fireman's Tournament held in Babylon and again hosted a fair on August 6th, 7th and 8th.

The V-8 engine was introduced to the world in 1915 and George Bunce was elected Chief. The year began with talk about the purchase of a pumping engine, a project that was ultimately rejected. It was decided, however, to have all the motor trucks painted with the Centerport Fire Department insignia. 1915 also saw the installation of a much-needed hot water heating system in the Firehouse.

Chief George Bunce
1915-1920

George Bunce was Chief, in 1916 a year spent dealing primarily with financial matters for the Department. Attorneys were hired to determine the need for Fireman's Compensation Insurance, the men were reimbursed for their uniforms and the janitor's wages were increased. In addition, rubber raincoats and a sterling silver fire alarm were purchased. In 1917, the inventor of the Speedometer, J.K. Stewart, purchased the estate of Austin Corbin, the President of the Long Island Railroad. This is where Mariner's Court is located today. The estate ultimately burned to the ground in 1960.

During the course of 1917, bids were requested for coal, the New York Telephone bill totaled $3.30 and the LILCO bill topped out at $2.00. George A. Bunce remained as Chief and the Assistant Chief was Percy Cross, who later resigned from the Department. In 1918, again, George Bunce was Chief with Walter Rowland as Assistant. A 90-day furlough was authorized for those in good standing if the need arose for them to take time off.

1917 - a bus used by Firefighter Tom Utter
Right - WKV Boat House 1919 - courtesy of Vanderbilt Museum

The original Centerport Yacht Club - located on the harbor side of the Mill Dam Bridge
Below - The Yacht Club and The Grist Mill

The era was known as the Roaring Twenties. With the passage of the 18th amendment, the Nation was "dry". That is, at least as dry as homemade liquor could be. Producing moonshine and rum running became new occupations and life was fast. Some of Centerport's local restaurants where rumored to have underground tunnels and trap doors under the bars! Automobile racing came into vogue as World War I was winding down. Americans spearheaded the industrial revolution that started in Europe and would soon become the leader of the industrialized world. Immigrants flowed through Ellis Island and passed the Statue of Liberty. Ahead emerged the skyscrapers of New York City and their gateway to the New World.

William K. Vanderbilt was the great grandson of a former immigrant and was known, as was his grandfather, as the "Commodore". He chose Little Neck Road in 1907 for his summer residence. It wasn't until the twenties, however, that it grew into a place of prominence. William was a man who loved adventures, from world travels to hunting, fishing and motor car racing. With the help of modern technology, he was able to have his own world class yacht and a seaplane for which he built a boathouse

Yacht Club and the Post Office (located on the pond side of the

One of Centerports first motorized pumpers - Photo Jim Feeley

and a seaplane hanger. This structure included quarters for the pilot and an electric generator. In 1922, he built a one-story structure, which was called the Marine Museum. Little did the Chief and the men of the Department know that this would become a very familiar place to them. Due to the size, it became necessary for the Department to be completely familiar with the layout of the structures, the placement of the private water works and hydrants, and the overall ins and outs of the complex in order to protect the estate adequately. To this day, the Department regularly holds drills and familiarity tours.

George Bunce was Chief and Walter Rowland was Assistant Chief. The Department, at this time, had few pieces of fire equipment and Chief Bunce became the driving force behind the purchase of

This Page Sponsored By:

Carl & Patricia Caiola and Family

Chief Walter Rowland
1921-1926

an American LaFrance chemical truck. This purchase occurred after fires destroyed the Denton estate house and a barn and chicken house on the Cobb estate. Around the same time Centerport assisted Northport with a fire that eventually destroyed the old opera house.

A close comradeship had developed over the 25 years since the Department was formed and now the wives wanted to become a part of the Department. A vote was taken and the Ladie's Auxiliary was formed. New Years Eve parties were held regularly, as were spring dances. In conjunction with the 25th Anniversary all Ex-Chiefs were given gold badges. Charter members, James Bunce and Walter Rowland, received 25-year pins at a special covered dish supper celebrating the anniversary.

In 1924, the Statue of Liberty was dedicated as a national monument on Liberty Island along with Ellis Island. Prior to 1924, the Department had functioned as a wholly independent corporation that relied on donations for its existence. In August, the Centerport Fire Department created a Board of Fire Commissioners in accordance with a State Law option. This was something not all fire departments chose to do. It consisted of five members, all of whom were active firemen, and would be known as the Centerport Fire District Incorporated. This move took a group of volunteers with some fire equipment and started to shape them into the professional well-equipped fire-fighting unit they were to become. This was necessary as Centerport was coming into a modern industrial revolution era and could no longer deal with "Mrs. Murphy's cow" burning down the whole town. The original Commissioners were George Miller, Chairman Thomas Utter, George Bunce, James Bunce and Frank Suydam. At this historic August organizational meeting a resolution was passed to tax the District $13,000.00 and issue bonds based on the credit of the District. Fire apparatus and equipment was purchased with the funds. An additional $2,600.00 was to be raised by tax to pay for fuel, lights, telephone, insurance, janitor salaries, building and apparatus maintenance and supplies.

The Fire District monthly meetings began in September. The first meeting was held specifically to arrange the transfer of the Fire Department property, apparatus and equipment to the District. The Commissioners also

Vanderbilt's Hall of Fishes - completed in 1922 - a second story was added in 1929 (The roof was the first tee of his golf course)
Photo courtesy of The Vanderbilt Museum

![Centerport Fire Department's 1926 Drill Team photograph]

Centerport Fire Department's 1926 Drill Team

read the Department by-laws and recommend changes. At the October District meeting, a motion was carried to purchase an American La France 400 gallon per minute Pumper for $8,500.00. At the November meeting, funds were approved for the purchase of 500 feet of hose from Eureka. The subject of converting the Ford chemical truck to a hook and ladder chemical truck was also discussed. The conversion was approved at the December meeting at a cost of $2,900.00. In five short months, the Fire District was becoming a modern fire-fighting unit. In 1925, the Commissioners requested a phone be installed in the Chief's house and asked the taxpayers for a tax increase in order to bring in a water supply. Things were changing and one had to wonder what would be next.

The hydrants and water mains that exist today were, of course, not always there. Route 25A had a small, galvanized main, as did Little Neck Road. Main Street in Northport and others were made of wood, while still others were made of steel or lead. Huntington Beach and Denton Hills had two-inch galvanized mains that were above ground. These had to be drained each winter as they served a summer community and would freeze in the winter. Thomas Utter was Chief and Edward Miller was Assistant Chief, in 1926, when standpipes were installed along the Mill Dam and around the pond. These standpipes can still be found but are no longer functional. The Department also passed a motion to blow the fire whistle once at 8am when school was going to be closed. The time has

This Page Sponsored By: Suffolk OB/GYN Group

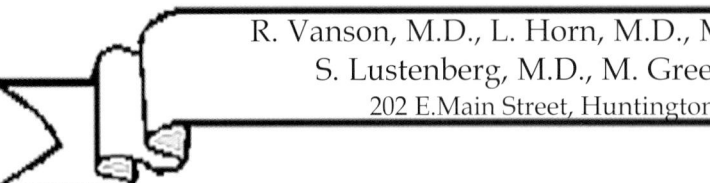

R. Vanson, M.D., L. Horn, M.D., M. Kramer, M.D.,
S. Lustenberg, M.D., M. Greenstein, D.O.
202 E.Main Street, Huntington 271-4330

Chief Thomas Utter
1927, 1929-1931

since changed to 7am, but the tradition is still carried on today.

The Fire Department, while no longer responsible for fire equipment, kept the tradition of receiving donations from the local community. These funds were used for the good and welfare of the volunteers, which included sports activities and promoting good will between the Fire Departments in the area. The Department also held a community fair, complete with booths and a raffle for a \$490.^{00} Chevrolet. Modern technology was getting its grip on Centerport. Dr. Robert Goddard, in Amherst Massachusetts, launched a rocket that traveled 184 feet in 2.5 seconds. The "boys" wanted to see if they could do as well on the ground so they passed a motion to buy a speedwagon for motorized drill competition. It cost \$110.^{00} With all this modern technology and the automobile at their disposal, they elected to go to Brooklyn to parade in the annual Washington's Birthday celebration. This was to become a regular event for many years to come.

In 1927, Edward Miller was Chief and Centerport started to grow and become a name on the map. Why? One reason for this notoriety seemed to be that the "World" was coming to Billy and Anna Linck's newly opened restaurant, Linck's Log Cabin, which drew 10,000 people a week in its heyday. Linck's was located on 25A just west of the pond on the corner of Centershore Road. Recently town houses were built on the site. Assistant Chief Harold Suydam participated at the big fire of the year, which totally destroyed Jack's Coffee Nook. William K. Vanderbilt divorced his first wife and then married Rosamond Lancaster Warburton. His world travel began in earnest after this new union. The original Fire Commissioners began to stagger the election process to insure that no more than one commissioner would be up for election each year. In 1927, Tom Utter and James Bunce were re-elected.

Modern technology "hit" again with the first television set and Centerport residents saw the opening of another new restaurant. The Water Mill Inn was opened by Fred Mueller in 1928 near Linck's on the North West Corner of 25A and Centershore Road and was billed as "The Rendezvous of Discriminating Patrons". After many name changes throughout the years, it is now a Chinese restaurant called Tung Ting. Huntington Beach was formed as a summer community on property bought by developers Hall and Ruhland from the Fleet and Irwin estates. People built cottages and made the seven-hour trip in their Model Ts or the more fashionable Model As. William K. added on to his estate once again by building a two-story Spanish style garage, complete with quarters for his chauffeurs. This building was also used as a Museum entrance and reception center and was added

This Page Sponsored By:

The Langel Family
56 Cherry Lane
Huntington, N.Y.

1928 - An aerial photograph of the Vanderbilt Estate / Little Neck Area
Photo courtesy of The Vanderbilt Museum

Chief Edward Miller 1928

to the fire-fighting plan and drills. The Department, under the direction of Chief Tom Utter, kept busy with ten good size brush fires and a house fire.

The Department went back to Brooklyn for another Washington's Birthday parade and the District allowed them to drive the apparatus to the parade. The newly established community of Huntington Beach asked the Commissioners for their own chemical truck due to the long distance from the Firehouse to their community. The truck was approved for purchase in 1929 and was manned by the local residents. The Roaring Twenties were winding down, as was the economy. America started on a downward economic spiral and as Centerport was not a haven for industry, many residents had to rely on the water and the land to make ends meet. Clams, oysters, potatoes and marketable goods were dinner supplements for many.

Today, Chiefs are elected, subject to the approval of the Fire Commissioners, for a one-year term. Customarily, they are re-elected for a second one-year term and their assistants follow suit. However, in the 1920s and 1930s, it was not, by any means, consistent. Some were elected for three or four years, some served non-consecutive terms and some were in office for only a few months. 1929 was Tom Utter's second of three years as Chief with Harold Suydam as his Assistant. The Great Depression hit and things worsened. Banks were failing and closing their doors throughout the nation. Not in Centerport, as there was no bank to fail. In fact, to this day, there has never been a bank located in Centerport. The nation's workers were being hit with higher and higher unemployment while one of the worst droughts in history hit the mid-west. Dust bowls were created where rich topsoil had been blown away due to the severe drought causing farm families to lose their land. Oklahoma was one of the hardest hit states and, after losing their farms, people moved, in desperation, to what they hoped would be greener pastures. Most of them, known as "Oakies", went to California.

Chief Utter did not have too many "saves" with fires this year. In August the Gucker family on Prospect Street lost their pump house, and, in November, the Vivadon house was also lost to fire.

The Commissioners actively enhanced the District. The chemical truck arrived and was commissioned, which created a new company

1929 - Centerport Garage on Centershore & Westfield
Photo courtesy of The Huntington Historical Society

1930 - Centerport's Chemical and Hose trucks

known as Chemical #2. A new Firehouse, to be built in Huntington Beach, would house it and residents of the area would man it. All meetings would still, however, be held at the main Firehouse. A membership quota of 65 was established and the 30 applications that had been received would be screened. With the new apparatus and company, a more widespread alerting system was needed and the Commissioners purchased gongs, which were located in Huntington Beach and Shorewood. The Commissioners also contracted with the New York Water Service Company to install water mains and hydrants in the District. They also agreed to pay Greenlawn Water for the use of their hydrants located in the District and to extend their mains to cover Laurel Hill.

The Department, prior to the District being formed, leased the land the Firehouse was on from the Town of Huntington for $1.00 a year. The District requested that the Town transfer the property to them. The request was denied on the grounds that since it was only $1.00 a year, there was no need for a transfer.

The new Chemical #2 building on Grant Street in Huntington Beach was dedicated on July 4, 1930 and the Huntington Beach firemen were ordered by the Commissioners to report to all fires within the District with the Ford chemical truck. At Chief Tom Utter's request, the Fire District started a Fire Police Company and purchased eight fire pumps, or Indian tanks, to be used at brush fires. Chief Utter, along with Walter Rowland, donated a Chevrolet and a Ford chassis to the District and the Chief offered to make the necessary changes to the truck bodies. At the same time, the District

placed an order for a #90 Brockway at a cost of $1,421.00 with an additional $42.00 for dual wheels, outfitting and lettering.

"Mutual aid" is the concept of fire departments helping each other out with large fires or when there may be a lack of manpower or equipment. Earlier in this century, it was not quite as organized. When one department called a neighboring department for mutual aid, sometimes everyone went. Today it is a very organized tool used effectively to handle large emergencies and is orchestrated through Town and County coordinators. In large emergencies, this coordination is extremely important in order to prevent the depletion of resources in a given area, leaving it unprotected. Mutual aid also includes "stand-by" whereby firefighters stay at a neighboring Firehouse in order to cover the area. Sometimes, however, even extra help will not defeat a fire. This was the case when Centerport was called by Halesite to help with a fire at the Fleet barn on Cove Road. Centerport responded with Assistant Chief Byron Nichols in charge, however, some time later, both Departments watched as the barn burned to the ground. Two other notable Centerport fires in 1930 included the Lockwood house, on Shore Road, which was totaled due to a gasoline-stove explosion and the Scudder's barn on Old Northport Road, which was also lost.

On a sad note, Centerport lost the life of Leon L. Lockwood, who was responding to a fire in Huntington Beach on Memorial Day, and was thrown from the fire truck. His was the only fatality the Department has suffered in its 100 year existance.

Modern technology "appeared" again in Centerport. In 1931 the Firehouse was converted from a coal furnace to an oil burner, which was what happened in most homes over the next 20 or so years.   The Fire Commissioners made a formal complaint to the Town of Huntington about the abandonment of old rusty cars on Prospect Street by St. Francis College, known today as Camp Alvernia, and about the congestion of cars parking east of Pataky's gas station/general store.

Vanderbilt's yacht the "Alva" - built in 1930
Photo courtesy of The Vanderbilt Museum

Pedestrians had to walk out on the Huntington-Northport Highway to get around not only this obstacle, but also the gas pumps, oil tanks and the clam stand. A similar complaint was lodged by the Halesite Fire Department, which addressed cars being left on the side of their Mill Dam Road. Was this the start of environmental and aesthetic values popular today? Tom Utter remained Chief and Byron Nichols was Assistant when Centerport started a baseball team. Ed Scherferstean and Byron Nichols were co-captains of this new team that practiced on the property of A. L. Field in Denton Hills. Chief Utter also organized a bowling team and created a committee, chaired by

Chief Byron Nichols
1932, 1937, 1945-1946

Harvey Smith, charged with reviewing the feasibility of forming a band. The Department came out with some new rules for members. Probationary firemen could not ride fire apparatus during their six months as a "probie". Also, to be a member, you had to be a permanent year round resident. Prior to this, the Department had allowed summer residents to join, but found it inadequate for training purposes. This rule was amended during World War II when manpower was at a premium.

The Fire Department Fair continued as an annual event and included the following booths in 1931: Cedar Chests, Groceries, Birds, Dolls, Luggage, Soda-Hotdogs, Klondike Mead, Lamps & Chairs, Blankets, Canes, Hoop-ala, Clocks & Watches, Throw Balls, Watermelons/fruit, Dance and, of course, the Big Six. A hefty profit of $2000.00 was realized.

The Depression was still a part of life and jobs were at a premium. The WPA created projects to try to keep people employed and some of the local roads are here today thanks to them. For instance, in 1932 the Huntington-Northport Highway (Route 25A) was resurfaced in concrete from Mill Dam Road to Stony Hollow Road and Little Neck Road going North still uses its original WPA concrete. In addition, most of the storm drains in Huntington Beach were the result of WPA projects. These have since been covered over with blacktop. Housing construction was booming and Lone Oak Drive of Denton Hills and the Little Neck area were well on their way. The Fire Department had a lot going on with fires and Departmental happenings. A big fire occurred in the Spring at the Northport Theatre, which was totaled along with two adjoining garages. Centerport was there on mutual aid and while the cause was unknown, the Chief cited a lack of water pressure as a contributing cause for the loss. He informed the District Attorney of this chronic problem, however, the DA said it was out of his jurisdiction. After helping Northport, Centerport had fires at the garage at The Maid's Rest Inn, the Abisher's house opposite the Crescent Club on the Main Road, Rosco Bishop's house, at the twin ponds on Northport Centerport Road and Mr. Jacob's house on Taft Circle, all of which were a total loss.

Muellers Water Mill Inn - Notice the water overflow on the left & Centershore Rd on the right

Chief Harold Witting
1933-1934

At the Firehouse, Doug Sammis and Tom Utter were appointed custodians and the band committee successfully organized a group that would include members, as well as junior members, who, of course could become active firemen when they came of age. In 1932, the generating station in Northport provided steady electric service and the first electric clock was purchased for the station. The annual fair was held again and a Chevrolet roadster was raffled for $.25 cents a chance.

It takes a lot for a fireman to rise from truck officer to Assistant Chief and, finally, to Chief. As a token of appreciation for their tireless volunteer service, the Department honored these men at a dinner. While thanking the outgoing Chief, the new Chief was recognized and wished well in his upcoming term. This was the start of the Installation Dinner, which is now a deep routed tradition in all departments.

The depression was winding down and things started to look brighter for many. The 21st Amendment repealed Prohibition in 1933 and people got on with their lives in a more "legal" manner. The WPA was still active and built a concrete roadway over the Mill Dam. At the same time, William K. Vanderbilt was becoming more of a community benefactor. Mr. Vanderbilt donated a new school on Little Neck Road since the old one, between the Firehouse and the Methodist Church, had become tired and undersized. Made of brick, it was the forerunner of the larger Centerport School on that site,

The Mill Dam Bridge in 1933

This Page Sponsored By:

DynaMed
6300 Yarrow Drive
Carlsbad, CA

which is now the Centerport Methodist Church. Tragedy struck William K. in 1933 when his son, William 3rd, was killed in a car accident. In 1936, he built an addition to his Eagle's Nest estate in his son's memory.

In 1933, Harold Witting was Chief and Doug Sammis Assistant Chief. Halesite called a mutual-aid in Knollwood Beach to stop a brush fire that spread to the cottage colony and destroyed two houses. Although the entire community was threatened, due to the efforts of both Departments, it was eventually saved. Just before the fire, the Commissioners suggested the Chief initiate a fire patrol service at fires to take charge of traffic and to keep outsiders out of harms way during fires. The Department formed a separate company, complete with officers, which is known today as the Fire Police.

The Department found itself in financial trouble partially due to larger than expected expenses in connection with the startup of the band. After much fuss and commotion, smoking was allowed at meetings. This was in effect until recently when Suffolk County prohibited smoking in all public places of assembly. With the smoking came a relaxation of a Commissioner's rule that prohibited games to be played in the Firehouse on Sundays. Honorary membership, treasured by some, was voted out by the membership. Those on the honorary rolls would have to join and become active firemen, or be dropped from the Department.

Harold Witting was in his second year as Chief and Harold Poplees was his new Assistant when, on February 2, 1934 Long Island was hit with the worst blizzard in years. Everything came to a standstill as people could not get out of their homes without shoveling out. However once they did, they could only walk to where they had to go. There were, thankfully, no emergency calls because it would have been difficult for the firemen to get to the Firehouse, let alone get the trucks on the road.

President Dr. John Reb
1934

As President Franklin Roosevelt's "New Deal" was unfolding and times were getting a little better, there were radios in half of all American homes, and the President was trying to get a "chicken in every pot". At this time, the Department decided to Incorporate instead of being a Company and the new concept of a President, Vice President, Secretary and Treasurer was introduced. New By-laws, required by the Certificate of Incorporation, were constructed. The Office of President was created in order to assist the Chief and to work with him in non-firematic matters. The Chief was in charge of drills, fires, and parades while the President was in charge of running the Corporation, which consisted of Department meetings, financial matters and fund raising. Dr. John Reb was appointed President at this time. Soon, the President also needed assistance and the office of Vice President was created. The existing Secretary and Treasurer were also under the President's jurisdiction. The financial recovery of the Department was credited to the President and other officers.

There were five fires of note in 1934. One, which happened at Hall's Inn, was the first fire reported by

tele-

The Fire Department in 1934

Chief Harold Poplees 1935

phone. Another fire involved most of the rear of Chester Mann's house on the Main Road, which was saved, even though it was fully involved when the Department arrived. Still another fire, this one also reported by phone, involved the outhouse behind a Lakeside Drive home. However, when the firemen arrived, they found the property destroyed. Also in 1934, the Hemlik house, on Laurel Hill, was destroyed and Charlie Martelli lost his two-story barn on Greenlawn Road.

1935 was a very quiet year both locally and globally. Harold Poplees was Chief with William McGrath as his new Assistant. There were no fires recorded for the year. Amazing, but true! 1936 was a more eventful year in Centerport and throughout the world. The groundwork for profound change was being formed. Adolph Hitler's army reoccupied the Rhineland, allegedly to reunite the German people, while, at the same time, Japan invaded Manchuria and set up a puppet state called Manchuoko. The Commissioners planned to meet with the School Board and the church to map out the turnover of a portion of the school property to the Fire District. They also partially answered a Department

President Henry Howe 1935

request to raise the maximum age limit for membership, from 35 to 45. The District, fearful of insurance complications approved 40 as the upper age limit. It remained there until recently when age discrimination became a prominent part of our lives. Now, rather than age as a deciding factor, the ability to perform the job is the key.

In the past, the Chief always took office on January 1st. In 1936, the Department changed this date to April in order to coincide with the new State standard for the beginning of the firematic year. That was not popular with some of the fire departments, so the State made it optional. Today, more than half the departments are on the regular January schedule while others use the April date. In Centerport, Harold Poplees became Chief with Ehardt Graulich as his Assistant, however, in April he resigned and Anton Polacek became Chief for almost two years.

The August Clam Bake started in 1936 and carried on for the next 35 years as a labor of love for the cadre of "experts" that cooked it. In brief, about 150 pieces of cheesecloth were cut up, then filled with corn, chicken

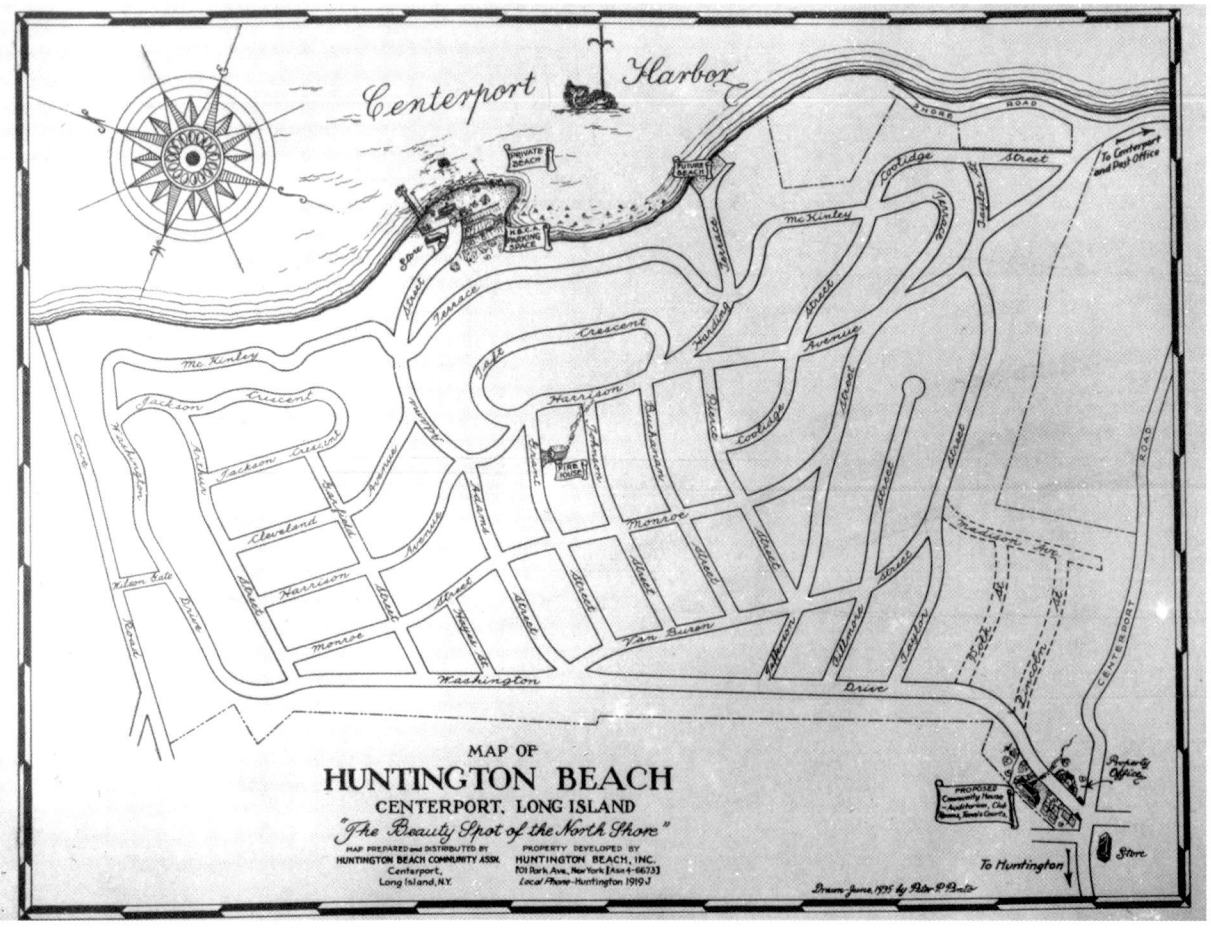

1935 - The new Huntington Beach Development - Photo courtesy of The Huntington Historical Society

Chief Anton Polacek Jr.
1936

and clams and then tied in a knot. As this was going on, a pit was dug behind the Firehouse and a bed of rocks was placed at the bottom. A large pile of cordwood was placed on top, ignited and allowed to burn down. Alternating layers of seaweed and baskets of the cheese-cloth packets were placed on the hot rocks and then everything was covered by a canvas and allowed to steam until done. Times changed, however, and soon the back of the Firehouse was covered with blacktop and no burning laws were enacted. It became harder and harder to find a spot to dig the cooking pit, so, after 35 years, the clam bake was changed to a summer cookout. The cookout was eventually cancelled due to budget restraints.

In November, Glynn's restaurant, at the curve of 25A and old Northport Road, suffered damage from a kitchen fire. Thanks to the help from Halesite Fire Department, a stop was made and most of the building was saved. Glynn's had many other fires in future years, one of which gutted more than half of the inside. Today, Viva Juan, a Mexican restaurant, exists on the site.

World tensions were growing and the dark clouds of war were on the horizon, yet, on the home front, it was relatively quiet. There were, however, a few recorded fires. The Ackerly house on Prospect had damage to a room due to an oil lamp that set the curtains on fire and, in Northport Harbor, a boat was lost to fire caused by a gasoline explosion. Gordon Soper was Assistant Chief in Chief Anton Polacek's year. At the Chief's request, the Commissioners agreed to purchase windshields for all the trucks. Windshields, at the time, were a thoroughly modern idea. Who ever thought a fire truck would have a windshield?

Around the world, the Spanish Civil War was heating up and Hitler and Mussolini were forming an alliance soon to be known as the Axis. In Centerport, Byron Nichols was Chief and Ehardt Graulich his Assistant. 1938 would prove to be a busy year for fires and for dealing with the worst hurricane to hit the area. A garage fire at Hyman's House on Shore Road destroyed both the structure and the car and damage was done to Offenkofer's church. The hurricane hit on September 21, the overall damage took weeks to clean up with three full days spent just clearing roads of debris and trees so emergency vehicles could pass. Manpower was at a

President Thomas Saunders
1936-1937

President Joeseph Moran
1938-1944

premium and the firefighters had to rotate shifts so they could all get to eat and sleep. At the low-lying areas many flooded basements had to be pumped out which was a job that was expected of the firefighters. Today it is no longer done on a routine basis.

A series of events began early in the year that led the way for a new Firehouse in Centerport. In February, the Board agreed to accept a parcel of land as a division between the Church property, which belonged to School District #7 and Mr. VanAlst was chosen as the architect for the project. In April, the District approved the architect's plan and presented it to the Department, which moved to accept the plan and also to look into turning the remaining fire apparatus and Department property over to the District. The District believed it was eligible for WPA funding for the Construction and proceeded to file the appropriate forms. The Commissioners expected a bond of $27,000.00 from the WPA, which was 45% of the estimated cost. Proposals, to purchase the property from the School District and construct and equip a Firehouse for an amount not to exceed $60,000.00, were presented to the public for a vote. The vote was overwhelmingly approved in

August. The Town of Huntington, which owned an adjacent parcel where the wooden Firehouse was, denied the Commissioner's request to turn the property over to the District. Instead, they would give the District a 50-year lease and suggested the Department turn over its present lease to the District, which was done.

Perhaps equally important to the firemen and the community as a new Firehouse was the formation of the first rescue squad in the Township of Huntington. Chief Byron Nichols proposed the idea of having a volunteer medical service for the residents to the membership in 1937. In 1938, the Commissioners approved the establishment of a first aid station in the Firehouse. With ten men who had passed their American Red Cross First Aid test, the Squad was formed with Al Kohler as Captain and Jack Thompson as Lieutenant. Two months after the founding of the Squad, the first ambulance was obtained. W.illiam K. Vanderbilt donated a 1938 Ford Panel Truck and First Aid Equipment to the Squad, (Department), who then turned it over the District. The newly formed Squad's first patient was Ex-Chief Ben Cairo of Northport. Over the last 60 years the Squad has developed into a fully trained company with about half the Department participating in its activities.

Chief Erhardt Graulich
1938-1944

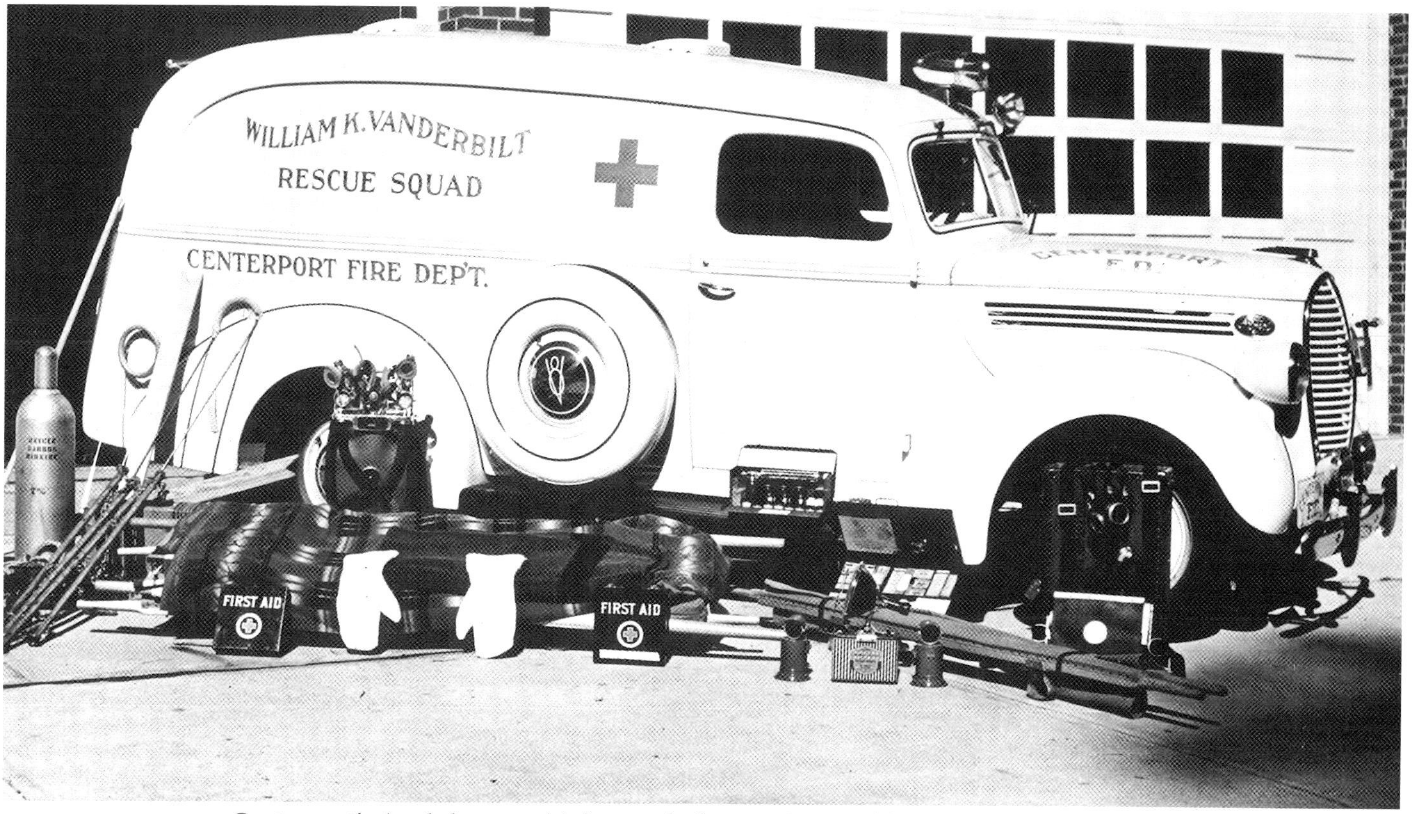

Centerport's (and the town's) first ambulance - Donated by William K. Vanderbilt
1938 Ford Panel truck

Its members have gone on to higher levels of training and have been instrumental in helping other Departments and the Huntington Community First Aid Squad get started. The Squad has seen many ambulances come and go and today, as a standard, it has two units available, each one capable of rendering Advanced Life Support, (ALS), when required. In 1938 it was the first and only ambulance in the Township, and they responded to many calls all over the Huntington area.

The theme of the 1939 New York World's Fair, held in Flushing, was "Peace and Freedom for the World of Tomorrow". How ironic considering that WW II had already begun with the invasion of Poland, France and Czechoslovakia by Germany and the world of tomorrow would be anything but peaceful. Ehardt Graulich was Chief and George Simpson was Assistant when the news arrived that Centerport was not eligible for the WPA grant. The cost of construction for the Firehouse was reduced from the original $60,000.00 to $45,000.00. Although Centerport had been playing softball for a while, the Huntington Township Softball League was first formed in 1939 with eight participating Departments. Centerport also had a team of regular Bowlers until the 1970s. Over the years, there had been many discussions

1940 - Firehouse construction and the dedication ceremony on October 8th

Above - Mr & Mrs Vanderbilt at the dedication
Right - Taking down the sign. This sign is currently on display in our museum.
Photos courtesy of The Huntington Historical Society

and/or arguments, regarding the cost of bowling and the percentage players had to contribute. While softball was basically free except for the cost of membership, balls and bats, the bowlers had to pay to use the alleys. The Department found the cost too steep and the guys some years had to kick in $.25 or $.50 per game.

1940 was a big year for the District. John N.R. Smith, a charter member of the Department, did ground breaking on the new Firehouse. In September there was a dedication ceremony and a parade around the Mill Pond. Victor Stukalo, Chairman of the Board of Fire Commissioners, invited the Town Supervisor, Arthur Kreutzer, William K. Vanderbilt and his wife to attend. The members of The Ladies Auxiliary, led by President Elsie Kohler, were also in attendance. In addition, at the same ceremony, the new ambulance, donated by the Mr. & Mrs. Vanderbilt, was

dedicated. Chairman Stukalo was very proud that the Firehouse came in at $40,000.00, which was $5,000.00 under the estimated cost. The Commissioners also approved the Department's request to increase the manpower cap from 65 to 100 members. The District now had to find a way to get rid of the old Firehouse and the siren tower. Originally, they decided to sell the tower to the Kings Park Fire Department for $25.00, but later decided to give it to them. The old Firehouse was sold to Theodore Bittner for $201.00 instead of taking bids for its demolition.

1940 One of the last pictures in front of the original Firehouse
Lower picture courtesy of The Huntington Historical Society

While Chiefs Graulich and Simpson were busy putting out 32 brush fires this year, the new President, Joseph Moran, was trying to "get a grip" on the Department finances. Although a fair was held each summer, the profits it realized totaled less than $2,000.00. No wonder the bowling team had to chip in to bowl. President Moran was a strong organizer and the leading force behind the Department's move in the right financial direction. All can thank him for where the Department is today. He instituted the Fund Drive and was instrumental in starting the Benevolent Fund. Some of his brother firemen thought

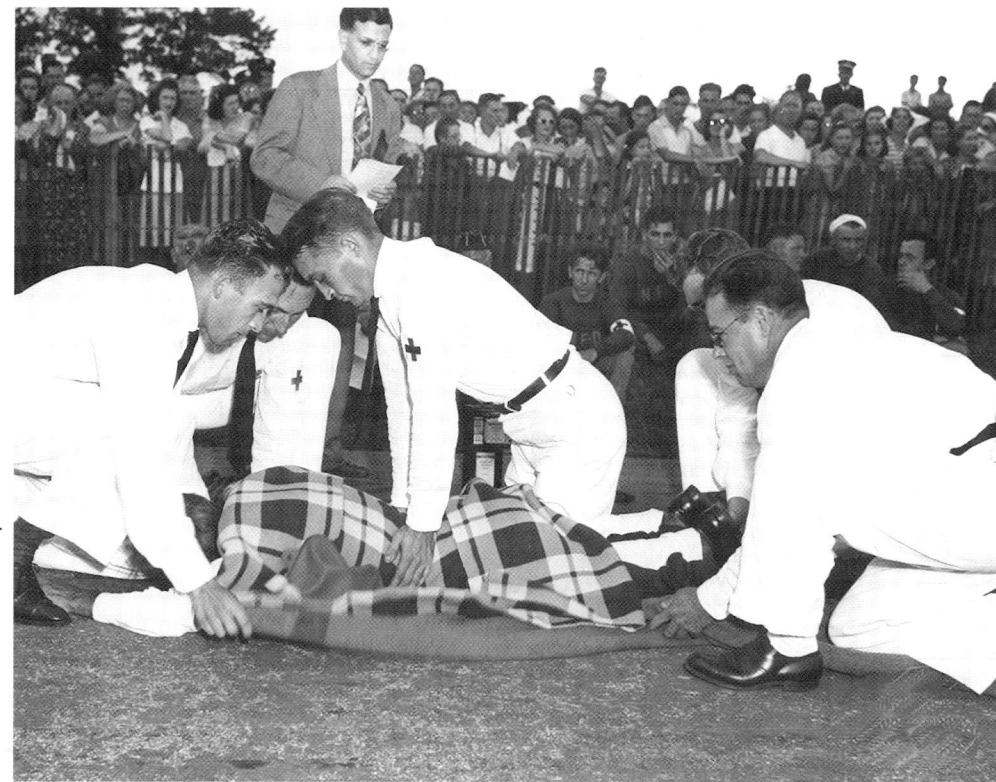

1940 -Cenetrport Rescue takes first place in the American Red Cross contest
L->R A. Kohler, O. Heinicke, G. Simpson, Dr. J. Reb, W. Swan
Photo courtesy of The Huntington Historical Society

so highly of him he was referred to as *Mr.* Moran. With the new Firehouse, the membership cap change, and the new Benevolent Fund guidelines, President Moran called for new By-Laws. At the May meeting, which lasted until 12:30am, the By-Laws were re-written. This was the longest Department meeting held to date.

That year the Firehouse was buzzing with gossip about a famous composer living on Little Neck. Sergey Vasily Rachmanioff rented a house on the Stewart Estate at the end of Mariners Court in 1940 and 1941 in order to rest and recuperate. After he left Russia in 1917, he lived in exile in the United States where he concentrated on his piano and conducting careers. During his stay in Centerport, he frequently played the piano and boats would gather in the water around his home to listen. He passed away on March 28, 1943 in Beverly Hills just days before his 70th birthday.

All officers stayed in place in 1941 while the world did not. The war in Europe had grown more aggressive and the U.S. aided its allies by sending supplies overseas. Then it happened! Pearl Harbor was attacked and the U.S. found itself at war in the Pacific. All of a sudden, bowling and other social activities became less popular at the Firehouse as the community braced for war. Although there were no significant fires recorded, there were many brush fires. Then, at the October meeting, reality set in as the discussion focused on the same topic discussed in all Firehouses: "Black

Above - The Thatched Cabin - on 25A
Left - Glynn's Inn - 25A/ Old Northport Rd
Below- 25A and Little Neck Road
All photos courtesy of
The Huntington Historical Society

Outs" and how to drill and practice with and for them. Many questions needed to be answered. How to put headlight shields on the cars? Who would the Air raid wardens, Fire Police, and Auxiliary Police be? After an attack like Pearl Harbor, anything could happen and the risks at home became clear. The U.S. could be bombed at any time and precautions needed to be taken.

The Chief officers stayed in place for 1942 as did the president and most line officers. The most significant fire of the year was at Glynn's Inn, which occurred on Christmas Eve. There is no information regarding the damage suffered. In line with the "Black Outs" the Commissioners agreed not to allow the issuance of fire permits for the duration of the war in accordance with the "Black Out" guidelines. Today, the Fire Inspector has strict guidelines to follow governed by the State's Anti-Pollution laws. In 1942 there were no such restrictions. The headlight blackout

shields also became applicable to fire apparatus and the Commissioners approved the purchase of "Black Out" shades for fireman's homes. Also, with the Chief's authorization, a fireman was allowed to purchase up to six gallons of additional gasoline each month, if used to respond to fires and emergency calls. This was figured on the base of 6 gallons equals 90 miles.

Men were going off to war and the ranks of the Department were thinning. The Chief asked the Board to allow the creation of an auxiliary fireman whose duties and direction were to be left up to the discretion of the Chief.

The impact of the war touched everyday life, however, life did go on. Nineteen members of the Department joined the military and a service flag was created with a star for each man serving. Additional stars were purchased, as, it was felt, more members would be leaving. The Department also decided to send a $5.00 money order as a Christmas gift to each of the Department members in the Armed Forces. With manpower tight, the chief officers stayed in place another year (1943). Bob

Geides Inn and Linck's Log Cabin - 2 very popular restaurants
Photos courtesy of The Huntington Historical Society

Bohaty was given permission to plant a victory garden on the Department property and the corner of Shore Road (Main Street), and Westfield Drive. Department apparatus was aging and the LaFrance chemical truck was falling apart so the Chief asked for a new pumper. This new generation of fire truck was a motor apparatus with a pump attached and would eventually replace the chemical truck. During wartime a new fire truck was not that easy to acquire as there was a nationwide freeze on the Production of all non-military vehicles. The Commissioners had to petition the War Priority Board, for a new truck and show cause why it was a priority. The Commissioners requested a Mack Type 80 combination pumper, as they did not have much choice. The approval came with an AA5 priority rating and with the stipulation that there be no extras on the truck. There was a public referendum with a decision of 41 to 0 in favor of the new pumper. The new pumper would be a 750 GPM triple combination at a cost of $8,800.00.

The new pumper arrived in 1944 and looked very bare without any chrome and with the head-light rims painted deep red. As years went by, it was discovered that the truck was almost a one-of-a-kind as only five were made during the War. Centerport's pumper came from Mitchell Field and was the largest pumper in the Township for about fifteen years.

The new Engine 1 - a 1944 Mack

The same Chief Officers were, once again, at the helm. Chief Graulich, however, had to resign in June due to a move out of the District. Before he left, though, he had the honor to receive a swan to be mated with a lone female on the pond. The story is "famous" and involves a swan and cygnet that lived on the pond. The male was mysteriously killed and Gracie Allen, of the Burns & Allen radio show, having heard about the incident from an article that appeared in the Brooklyn Eagle, told the show's sponsors, Swan Soap. The sponsors called the Firehouse to announce Gracie was sending a swan to replace the one killed. The story goes that Bill Swan answered the phone putting the caller in a state of shock. The new swan was sent via American Airlines and Chief Graulich got his picture in the papers as he received the swan from an

airline stewardess at LaGuardia. "Sadie" was put in the Mill Pond to meet her new mate "Clarence". This was done amidst many fanfares as almost all of Centerport turned out for the event, which was covered by the Herald Tribune. As it turned out, the two birds never became good friends as Clarence attacked Sadie almost immediately. Swans mate for life and, unfortunately, our Sadie was banished to the opposite side of the pond.

With so many men in the military, the District allowed the Department to drop the admittance age to 16 years of age. This allowed about ten new members to join, almost all of whom stayed in town and in the Fire Department to eventually become life members. In September, the hurricane of '44 hit and the men went into action again clearing roads and pumping out basements.

President Alfred Harris
1945-1948

Although not as crippling as the 1938 hurricane, the Department had to also contend with a number of brush fires and air-raid drills. Does anyone remember what "Red signals", "White signals" and "Blue signals" were?

On a sad note, William K. Vanderbilt I, the man they called "A Renaissance Man" passed away in the fall. He died of a heart attack at his Park Avenue residence at the age of 65. William K. was a good benefactor and friend to both Centerport and the Department and his legacy remains in the current Firehouse and the former Little Neck School, which is now the Centerport Methodist Church. Before he died, he offered a sizable endowment to the Fire Department if they would change their name to the "William K. Vanderbilt Centerport Fire Department". Centerport declined the offer and kept its original name.

In his will, Mr. Vanderbilt left his Centerport estate, which included a trust fund of two million dollars to care for it and the condition that his wife would be allowed to remain in residence until she died. Eagle's Nest was actually left to the Town of Huntington who declined it. Suffolk County accepted the terms and, although it had serious growing pains as a public entity, it is today a proud part of Centerport and its history.

What a year 1945 was. The Marines landed on Iwo Jima and Okinawa, President Franklin Roosevelt died of a cerebral hemorrhage, Vice President, Harry Truman became President and, on May 7, known as VE-Day, Germany surrendered. The war in the Pacific continued, however, and, in August, President Truman gave the order to drop atomic bombs on Hiroshima and Nagasaki. Japan surrendered on August 15, known as VJ-Day, and World War II was finally over. Everyone looked forward to seeing his or her loved ones return home. The Fire Department expanded its Chief officer and Department officer titles as responsibilities increased. Byron Nichols was Chief with George Simpson his First Assistant, and George's brother Arthur Simpson as Second Assistant. In the Department the office of Second Vice President, Assistant Secretary and Assistant Treasurer were created to help with the ever-expanding business end of the Department. One of the largest fires on record happened in the spring when the Van Iderstine mansion, on Little Neck Road, burned down. Even with the Greenlawn Fire Department assisting, six Centerport firemen were treated for minor injuries at Huntington Hospital.

This Page Sponsored By:

Halesite Fire Department
1 North New York Avenue
Halesite N.Y.

Centerport's
Front Line
in the 40's

The War caused fundamental changes in the society, which required adjustments for everyone. Women had entered the workplace during the war in defense plants and in other areas where there was a shortage of men. "Rosie the Riveter" was born and did not want to go away. She even started wearing a bikini bathing suit. Many women stayed in the workplace and some did want to leave to start a family. A building boom began and developments, such as Levittown, sprung up and, soon after, the "baby boom" exploded. Families took advantage of the G. I. Bill that allowed veterans an opportunity to get a higher education and colleges expanded. A new breed of educated professionals entered the workplace, which forever changed the American way of life.

In 1946, the slate of officers was re-elected, the Commissioners sold the American LaFrance for $275.00 and started looking towards the future. A 20-year plan was adopted and an apparatus replacement fund was started with $3,500.00 earmarked in the 1947 budget and in subsequent budgets. This move was partially due to the certification requirements of the Fire Underwriters who would certify a pumper by, among other things, its pumping capacity.

On a sad note, Ashley Thompson, one of the 19 members

Chief George Simpson
1947-1948

1947 - Motor Vehicle Accident (MVA)
Photo by Peter Vanalst

Kenneth Klerk
"Ken"
Fire Police
June, 1948
Chief Emeritus: 1993
Chief: 1968-1969
1st Asst. Chief: 1966-1967
2nd Asst. Chief: 1964-1965
Engine Co. #1:
Captain: 1962-1963
Lieutenant: 1960-1961
Rescue Squad: 1963-1985
E.M.T.: 1972-1980
Commissioner: 1970-1990
Huntington Fire Chiefs' Council
President: 1965-1966
Huntington Fire District Officers'
Assn.
President: 1984-1986

Earl Sammis

Eagle Truck Co. #1
November, 1948
Chief: 1958-1959
1st Asst. Chief: 1956-1957
2nd Asst. Chief: 1955-1956
Hose Company:
Lieutenant
Chemical Company:
Captain & Lieutenant
Hook & Ladder:
Captain and Lieutenant
Service Company:
Captain & Lieutenant
Engine Co. #1:
Captain & Lieutenant
Rescue Squad: 35yrs
Chief Emeritus
Advanced First Aid: Past

who served in the War, died in the line of duty. He is pictured, in his uniform, on the Firehouse wall. A memorial was started in his name for the best fire prevention essay written by the school children, with an award given yearly.

In 1947, George Simpson became Chief and his brother Artie Simpson moved up to First Assistant. Newly elected Joseph Jaret became Second Assistant. Aside from Link's Log Cabin having its first of numerous fires and the Commissioners ordering a new Chevrolet truck with a 350 gallon booster pump, nothing of significance was recorded. The adjustment period after the war continued. A Membership Committee, which consisted of five members, was created by the Department to screen applicants for membership. The Committee's approval was needed before a prospective member could be voted on by the membership. However, prior to the Membership Committee interviewing a person, an applicant had to have a sponsor. Voting was done by the black ball system, a practice common to most organizations at the time. This was a secret ballot and if a person received three black balls he was not admitted. The President or Secretary announced the results of the ballot. The saying, "The ballot box is clear" indicated there were no black balls and the person was admitted to membership. Years later, this system was changed and a majority vote by paper ballot was instituted.

It was a cold winter and the Mill Pond was frozen. Skaters stayed in the "Safe" areas, however, there were spots where the ice was thin and, therefore, potentially dangerous. The Department took on the responsibility of hanging life rings and ropes in the "Safe" areas, a practice, which lasted for years until more sophisticated and organized methods of rescue were in place.

In the spring of 1948, the body of Ashley Thompson was returned home from overseas. The Department held a funeral service for him at the Firehouse. This brought a certain amount of closure to the Department regarding the war. Memories linger on, however, and people never really forget. Karl Marusak, a current member of the Department frequently recalls his own experiences while serving in Pearl Harbor during the air raid.

The LP record and Polaroid camera hit the market announcing another addition to the modern age. The Centerport Fire Department was 50 years old and had witnessed so many changes through the years. New fire trucks, windshields, a modern brick Firehouse, and the telephone were among the many innovations the Department saw in its half century of serving the community. A committee was set up, at the suggestion of Joe Moran, to have a celebration to mark the 50th anniversary.

On the world front, trouble was brewing. There is no exact date to mark it and there was no bombing, invasion or declaration, yet the Cold War was about to begin. The Union of Soviet Socialist Republics blockaded the allied sections of Berlin, so the U.S. and Great Britain airlifted more than two million tons of food and coal to aid the Berliners.

Modern technology struck again in 1949 as television grew nationally and the 45 rpm records came

Chief Joseph Jaret
1949-1951

President Harry Pearsall
1949-1951

This Page Sponsored By:

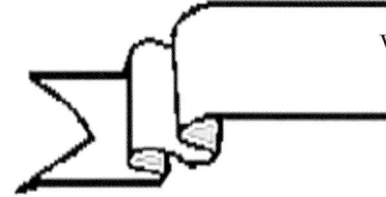

Vincent & Lorraine Vaneck & Family

of age. Tom Utter asked for a vote to approve the purchase of a television set for the Firehouse. The members voted in favor of the purchase and the Firehouse had telephones, lights, modern fire equipment <u>and</u> a TV. The first program watched was The Arthur Godfrey Show and everyone got a big kick out of it. The Department sold its property on Lakeside drive to a Department member who, offering $1,100.00, was the highest bidder. There was no mention as to the identity of the new owner. Joe Jaret was elected Chief with Bill Wamp Sr., First Assistant and Richard Reynolds as Second Assistant. Chief Jaret was a forward-looking person and a great politician. 1949 was the year the Commissioners increased their budget for such things as the new apparatus replacement fund and for $3000.00 to improve the grounds and parking area. These items were approved unanimously. Improving the parking area, however, meant adding blacktop to the rear of the Firehouse, which decreased the available space for digging a clambake hole. The beginning of the end was at hand for the annual August Clam Bake.

The cold war got quite a bit colder and the U.S. pulled all of their diplomats out of China in 1950 after an attack on its embassy in Peking. Soon after, with the help of China, North Korea invaded South Korea, crossing the 38th parallel. The United Nations tried to work out a cease-fire but their efforts were ignored. It then urged all member nations to join in and bring the invasion to a halt. President Truman responded by ordering the U.S. Air Force and Navy to assist. Within days, air strikes were started against North Korea as U.S. and British troops joined in the action. On the home front, people started to buy color TV sets as the national networks started transmitting a few shows in color. The NBC Peacock was about to be "hatched". About this time, Chief Jaret became instrumental in developing an innovative program of training new firemen in the District. In the past, most training was done on an informal basis with new members first watching and then participating with experienced firemen in firematic maneuvers. They were expected to familiarize themselves with the trucks and all of the equipment. The fireman's job, at the time, was strictly learned by experience. Chief Jaret's idea was for a more organized training program. This was, in essence, an early version of what is now a mandatory probie (probationary) school conducted throughout the county.

Every year, the State of New York Fire Chief's Association and the Fire District Association hold an informative seminar in various locations around the State. For the most part, Centerport attended if economically feasible. 1950 marked a first when the fire District Association seminar, normally attended by the Commissioners only, was held in New York City and authorization was given for the Commissioners, Fire Inspector, firemen and apparatus to attend. The cost was not to exceed $6.00 per day per man. This never happened again, however, and attendance reverted back to Commissioners only.

In 1949, the Commissioners voted to approve the purchase of a new ladder type fire truck. In 1950, a referendum was held and by a slim margin of four votes, an expenditure of up to $18,000.00 was approved, with some of the money coming from the apparatus replacement fund. Buildings were getting taller and the longest ladder extended only 20 feet. This new truck allowed the Department to carry longer ground ladders. In October, an American Fire Apparatus combination ladder

Dutchess - The Department Dog

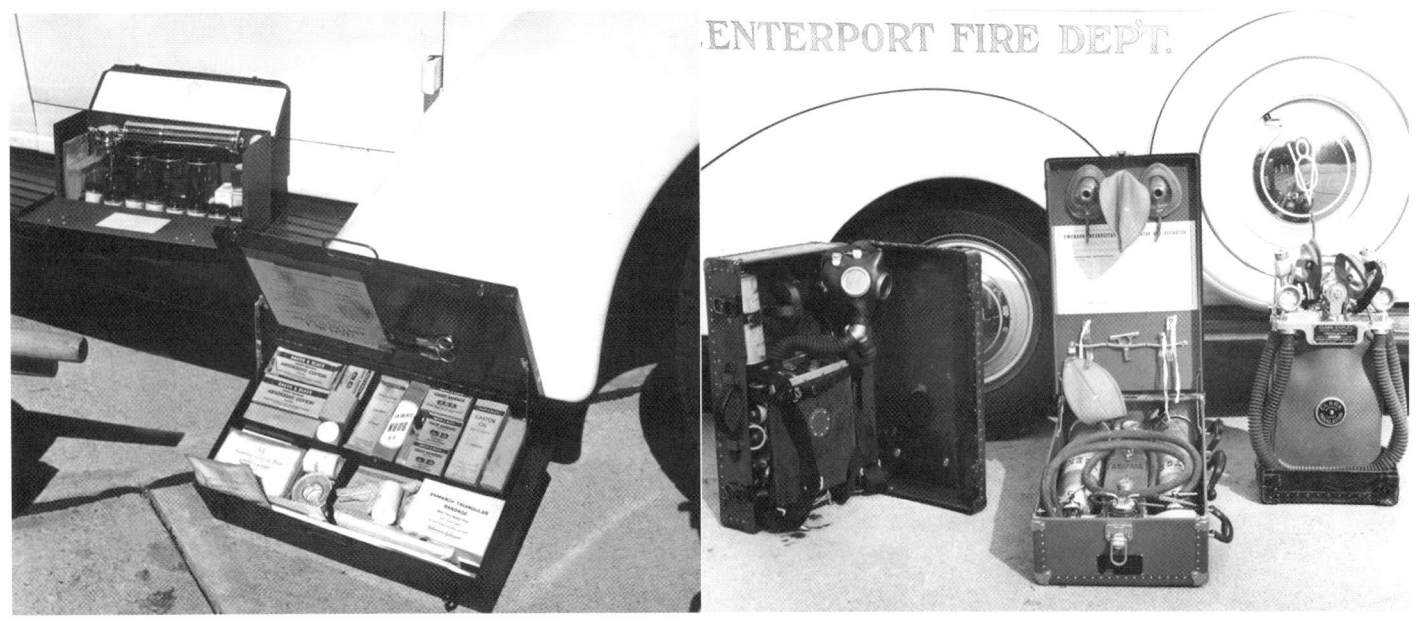

Modern Rescue Equipment in the 1950's - These can be seen in our museum now

and pumper with a booster was purchased at a cost of $17,125. The addition of this vehicle resulted in a morale boost for all of the firemen, especially for the Juniors. This truck evokes memories even today and was the subject of many stories over the years. The wonderful shift lever always allowed the driver to bash his knuckles against the dashboard when he shifted into third gear. Most proficient drivers palmed the lever up, which caused it to hit the dash with a bang. When it went around corners, riders wondered if all four wheels would stay on the ground for it was a bit top heavy with all the ladders fitting around the internal water tank. Then there was the Bangor ladder. It had five sections and two outriggers to be manually placed on the ground so it would not collapse when extended to its full 50 feet. Extending it was a two man pulling operation, while two other men handled the outriggers. Two more men held it upright while pulling and everyone else just prayed. As years went by, Departments acquired motorized ladders, which made life a little less hazardous for the firefighters. The truck itself was a good piece of fire fighting apparatus and one of its major work savers was its four-stage pump. Three stages would normally be used with hoses, but the fourth stage, used with its booster reels, would give enough pressure to create a fog mist, which was important when fighting brush fires. The 800 pounds of pressure dislodged brush and underbrush to expose fire that normally would have to have been dug and swept in order to gain access.

The Fire police also received a "new vehicle" in 1950. The old model "A" was restored and given to them and they used it with pride. They bounced around the District in it during the cleanup after the big storm on November 25. The entire Department participated in the cleanup and the pumping out of basements. Chief Jaret was very thankful for the efforts of all the men and the Ladies Auxiliary. The Department band that was, in the past, combined with Greenlawn, due to expense and lack of participation, had mysteriously returned to Centerport.

1951 was a very quiet year. Not much was written about it. The Chief Officers remained the same

This Page Sponsored By:

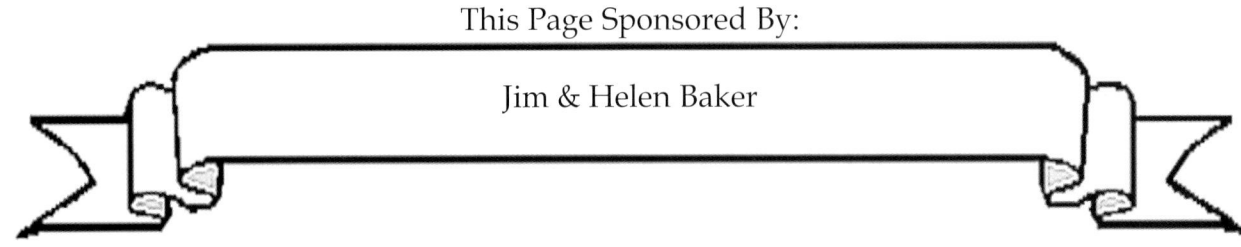

Jim & Helen Baker

Centerport Harbor in the 50's
Photo courtesy of Camp Alvernia

with the exception of Bob Gangloff who replaced Rich Reynolds as Second Assistant Chief. Bob Bohaty was President and, for the twenty- fifth year, Franz Kellogg served as Treasurer. In appreciation for his continuous dedicated service, the Department presented Franz with a watch. The Treasury was slowly and steadily growing and Franz attributed some of it to the ever growing success of the annual August Fair. The Fair was now something the community and many others from outside Centerport counted on as part of their summer vacation enjoyment. By now the community had grown considerably and included not only summer residents, but also many year round home owners. Some commuted to the city while others found local Long Island jobs. The Parkways were extended and improved in order to make travel easier and weekenders came out to their recently winterized summer bungalows in Huntington Beach and Denton Hills. As fast as the community was growing, television was growing faster. The TV became very popular, 13 million TV sets were in homes, which was ten times the number in 1950.

William A. Wamp, Jr.
"Bill"
Engine Co. #2
February, 1952

Chief Emeritus
Chief : 1979, 1981
2nd Asst. Chief:
1968-1969

Engine Co. #2:
Captain 1965-1967
Lieutenant: 1963-1964
Rescue Squad: 1953-1973
Advanced First Aid:
Past

The tournament team was trying to get its feet off the ground. The old hand pulled hose wagon had just been refurbished and was used in the tournaments. Captain Bob Gangloff noted that the ranks were low and more help was needed. At this time, Huntington elected to stop the motorized tournaments typical of other townships and just stay with the "old fashioned" and safer style of contest. The Rescue Squad elected to attend a State tournament in New York City where they placed sixth. They received a cash prize and Earl Sammis suggested it be put in the Benevolent Fund. It was done and a

This Page Sponsored By:

Bea & Joe Carillo

President Robert Bohaty
1952-1953

committee was appointed to oversee the fund.

George Simpson, Captain of the Rescue Squad, started a procedure that is still carried on today. It was difficult to rely on people showing up for evening and/or night rescue calls, so he instituted a system of having four members on call each night. They were responsible for being available on the night they chose and had to find replacements in the event of a conflict. It was later refined to the point where a person on call had to verify with the dispatcher that he was ready, willing, and able for duty.

Centerport was expanding and more and more people were staying year round, which was characteristic of all shoreline communities, both on the North and South shores, of the Island. However, the center of the Island was undeveloped and still heavily forested. Brush fires were common in Centerport, but were usually of little consequence. When brush fires started in the center of the Island, however, they could easily turn into forest fires and take days to extinguish. Such was the little brush fire that started in Dix Hills around May 1st,1951. It only took a few hours before it was heading toward Brentwood and the forested grounds of Pilgrim State Hospital. For days, 500 men from 25 Departments fought the blaze. At one point, three men from Brentwood were ordered to go into a burned out area and start a backfire. Winds, however, carried the blaze over into their area and they never had a chance to start the backfire. One of the three injured men died two days later and another died the following week. The third survived, although he was severely burned. Chief Bill Wamp, and his Assistant, Bob Gangloff were dispatched

Chief William Wamp
1952-1953

Douglas Davidson
Fire Police
June, 1952

Chief: 1970-1971
1st Asst. Chief: 1969-1968
2nd Asst. Chief: 1967

Fire Police:
Captain: 1995-1998
Hook & Ladder Co.:
Captain: 1960-1962
Lieutenant: 1958-1959
Rescue Squad: 1952 - 1977

Chief Robert Gangloff
1954-1955

President Robert Spence
1954-1955

with the Centerport contingent to help fight the fire. Assistant Chief Gangloff brought a donation to the Brentwood Firehouse for the fund that was established for the deceased firemen. He also brought a donation of food for their families and visited the surviving fireman. A memorial monument presently stands in front of the Brentwood Firehouse. Today there are funds established for tragic mishaps, such as this, in order to help a fireman's family.

Richard Reynolds was our Second Assistant Chief when the membership structure was changed. The active rolls contained many "Old Timers" or inactive firemen who did not want to retire for fear they would lose their benevolent benefits. This was during a time when a member had to be active in order to belong to the benevolent, which created a waiting list for membership that did not move very quickly. In order to get more participating fireman, and not discourage those on the list in the process, the Department changed the quota of active men from 100 to 125. At the same time, the age parameters were established at 18 and 49. It's interesting to note that it was made very clear that these changes in membership parameters be confined to males only. It was during this time that "youngsters" like Doug Davidson and Bill Wamp Jr. became active.

1952 was another quiet year. The three chiefs remained in office as did all Department officers including President Bob Bohaty. The Rescue Squad was becoming more and more prominent and it was decided that the white panel truck, donated by William Vanderbilt, had reached the end of its cycle and a newer, more universally equipped standard ambulance would better serve the community. So after motions and approvals the District agreed to purchase a Cadillac ambulance which arrived in August and was put in service immediately. At the same time, the Ford rescue truck was also showing its age. The District was a little short on cash and the apparatus replacement fund cookie jar was empty so they had to borrow money to pay for the new and updated truck. This was one of the only times in the District's history that bonds were issued.

1953 was the first year since the formation of the softball league that Centerport won first place. The encouragement of the win was a catalyst and the team looked forward to future seasons and future wins. Records do not clearly indicate when it began, but there was an annual carol sing and tree lighting activity held every December. The Department would string lights on a large tree next door to the Firehouse at the Methodist Church. The men, Ladies Auxiliary and the community would all gather by the tree and wait for it to be lit and then the carol sing would commence. Following, all would be invited to the Firehouse for light refreshments and warmth. This tradition is still carried on today.

As the Korean War is ended, members serving in the military returned home. A resolution was passed that all men past, present, and future that serve in the military be given credit in the Department for time served. 1953 marked the year the Catholic parish of Our Lady Queen of Martyrs was founded. Church services were originally held in a boathouse that looked like an elongated garage, which was donated by Mrs. Brunswick and located where the present church parking lot is.

At the annual meeting in 1954, Robert Gangloff was elected Chief, Richard Reynolds his First Assistant and Earl Sammis became the new Second Assistant Chief. At the time, New York had three teams: the Brooklyn Dodgers and the New York Giants in the National league, and the New York Yankees in the American league. This generated a lot of interest in baseball and game attendance was at a high, as was team rivalry. The name "subway series" became a part of the culture. There was a great pennant race between the Dodgers and the Giants and a World Series win for the Dodgers in 1956. As the Fifties went on, we lost the Dodgers to Los Angeles and the Giants to San Francisco and baseball would never be the same in New York. While Rock and Roll was hot, the Cold War continued its cool down. The forces of Communism and Democracy were in a power struggle, which resulted in a great arms buildup on both sides. The U.S. launched the Nautilus, the first nuclear submarine, and Senator Joe McCarthy began holding congressional hearings into alleged communist activity within the U.S. borders. It was a time of tension and worry.

Civil Defense, a Federal program that guided towns and counties, became reactivated as fear of nuclear attacks increased. Huntington set up a Civil Defense Agency with liaison representatives for the fire departments. While no one knew exactly what devastation a nuclear attack might bring, people were reminded of the devastation in Japan from atomic bombs. In preparation for the worst, Advanced First Aid classes were held to train the men to treat patients in the event a doctor was not available. Civil Defense Drills were held throughout the Town and focused on schools where students were instructed on how to "run for cover". Certain key build-

Peter J. Reilly

Fire Police
December, 1953

Honorary Chief: 1994

Treasurer: 1955-1974

Fire Police:
Lieutenant: 1990-1991,
1994-1998

Harry R. Burr

Fire Police
September, 1954
Chaplain: 1966-Present

Chief: 1963
1st Asst. Chief: 1962
2nd Asst. Chief: 1961
Commissioner: 1976-1993
Secretary: 1958-1961
Rescue Squad: 1955-1993
Lieutenant: 1968-1969
Hose Company:
Captain: 1960
Lieutenant: 1958-1959
Past E.M.T

1954 - Patiky's Service Station - Little Neck & 25A

ings, mainly basements of public buildings, were designated as fallout shelters. Civil defense also ruled that fire apparatus, when used for civil defense, would be manned by eight men and an officer. The public fallout shelters led to the increasing popularity of home shelters. Some families designated a part of their basement as a safe place and stocked it with life sustaining supplies. Others were more aggressive and built separate fully equipped bomb shelters in their back yards to insure the safety of their families. The roll of the Fire Department expanded beyond that of assisting with Civil Defense. National Fire Prevention Week, established by Congress in the past, became more focused and required more. The Ashley Thompson Medal continued to be awarded for the best fire prevention essay, but now the Fire Departments were expected to teach fire safety in the schools as part of Fire Prevention Week. The schools set aside time for the firemen to visit with their apparatus and instruct the children on what the various functions of the trucks and ambulance were. Assemblies were also held, during which the Ashley Thompson Medal was awarded.

With all this stepped up first-aid training, the Rescue Squad became the first in Suffolk County to be recognized by the Suffolk County Medical Society, which was headed by Dr. Goodrich. Also, for the first time, the Squad had twenty-one men certified by the National Trauma Society. Captain George Simpson was responsible for all the training and for developing the Squad into the highly trained unit it was. George also trained the Department in the use of the new life saving net and was

This Page Sponsored By:

1955 - Memorial Day Picnic

instrumental in having life saving equipment placed at key locations around the Mill Dam water area. Such locations included Manaro's Market, Simpson's Boat Yard and the rear of the Firehouse. On a local level, everyone knew that if there were an attack or a disaster of any kind, blood would be a key factor. Centerport joined with the Northport Fire Department in the creation of a blood bank. Huntington Hospital purchased a bloodmobile and a regular schedule was instituted in Centerport or Northport for community members to donate blood. To insure the best response to alarms and Civil Defense Drills, the Commissioners installed new updated radios in the fire trucks and added two more sirens at the Vanderbilt Museum and the newly opened Washington Drive School, both considered key locations in the District. The Commissioners also agreed that the 125-man limit was no longer needed and the rolls were returned to 100 members, where the limit remains today. A new hose truck was purchased exclusively to haul hose to be stretched out from hydrants to pumpers or the quad ladder truck.

On a county level, training was becoming more focused. Yaphank was designated as the fire training headquarters for the Suffolk County and plans were drawn for a formal fire school training ground. The Department went on record, as did many others, to approve the plans and hoped for an early completion of the facility.

This Page Sponsored By:

Chief Richard Reynolds
1956-1957

In 1956, in the midst of the Cold War, the Harborfields School District was formed. In the Town of Huntington, as well as across the nation, the threat of nuclear war was still all too real. Air raid drills were still a common occurrence in classrooms, stores and private homes and the Centerport Fire Department continued to play a key role in these drills by sounding the siren. Residents knew, at the sound of this alarm, to carry out the procedures that were developed in case of a nuclear attack.

In 1956, the "Blue Light" became a privilege for all volunteer firefighters, accompanied by a card, first distributed in 1955. The use of this light would make it faster for the members to respond to calls, as other motorists would be alerted to the need to allow the firefighters to quickly reach the fire station. Firefighters were reminded, however, at the June meeting, to continue to respond to calls with caution. More and more cars were on the roads and although seatbelts were introduced to the public for the first time in 1956, society as a whole was not in favor of them.

In October, Centerport received honorable mention in the Daily News for their efforts in Fire Prevention Week, which was conducted by Fire Inspector Joseph Jaret. In the elementary and junior high schools, winners received ribbons as awards for the poster and essay contests. In Harborfields High School, an advanced essay contest was held and Fire Inspector Jaret awarded the Ashley Thompson medal to the winner.

During 1956, methods of storing and typing blood became very advanced. The Centerport and Northport Fire Departments continued to assist Huntington Hospital and the Bloodmobile in maintaining a blood supply that could be used at all times. Fifty donors were needed in any one location for a blood drive to be

President Anthony Priore
1956-1957

1957 - Automatic Alarm box

Conrad G. Zink
"Connie"

Fire Police
June, 1957

Service Company:
Captain: 1982
Lieutenant: 1981
Rescue Squad: 1961 - 1984
Secretary: 1960 - 1991
A.F.A. (past)
1997 Honorary Chief

effective so both departments worked together to make each blood drive a success.

On October 2, 1957 a new Mack hose truck was put into service. The Hose Company's job was to provide connections from the fire fighting apparatus to the hydrants. Brush fires were still quite prevalent with an estimated two to three calls a week. The undeveloped part of Little Neck Road was particularly susceptible to these types of fires. In November, an inter-departmental drill took place and among the 12 participating fire departments, Centerport placed second.

In 1957, the Cold War and weapons race was still in full force as the Soviets launched the first space satellite, Sputnik I. The United States caught up to the Soviets when the satellite Explorer I was launched in January of 1958. During this time, the New York City Police were trying to track down a "Mad Bomber" who was known for planting bombs in municipal buildings. The Town of Huntington Council of Fire Chiefs reported that schools were receiving a large amount of bomb scares and precautions were taken. Plastic was beginning to be manufactured at an enormous rate. Due to its potential toxic effects, fire departments were urged to familiarize themselves on the hazards of dealing with a fire in which plastics were possibly involved and to always use masks in these situations.

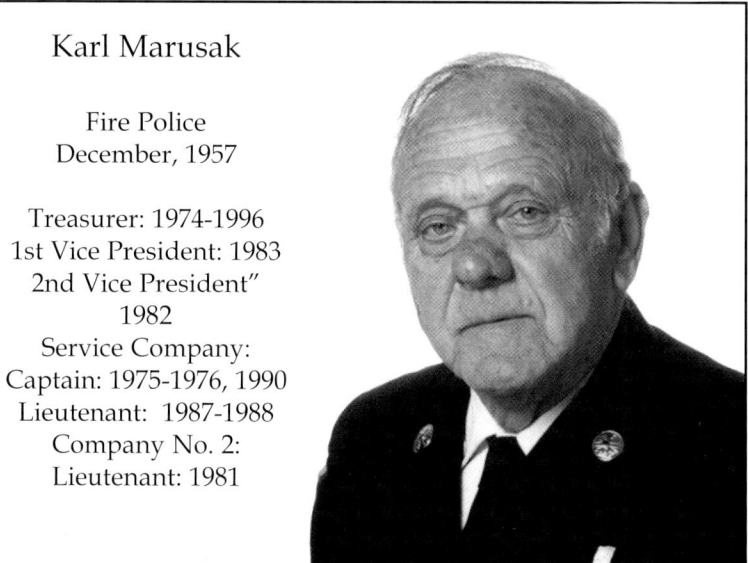

Karl Marusak

Fire Police
December, 1957

Treasurer: 1974-1996
1st Vice President: 1983
2nd Vice President"
1982
Service Company:
Captain: 1975-1976, 1990
Lieutenant: 1987-1988
Company No. 2:
Lieutenant: 1981

Ice Fishing (eels) on the Mill Pond
Photo courtesy of Harvey Weber

On September 21, 1959 Linck's Log Cabin was destroyed by a fire, which began at 2:45 AM in the kitchen. When Centerport Fire Department arrived at the scene under the direction of Chief Earl Sammis, it was fully involved. Many neighboring departments were called for mutual aid. It took almost two full days until the Department felt comfortable that the fire was completely out, and it was only then that the firefighters were relieved from their responsibilities.

The role of Fire Police, as discussed earlier, is another

Chief Earl Sammis
1958-1959

President Otto Heinicke
1958-1959

very important responsibility of the Department. To assist them in this role, a new police truck was purchased in June. The old Ford police truck was sold in August to Jerry's Service Center for $150.00. As the number of motor vehicles continued to increase and safety on the roads became more of an issue, Chief Sammis put into effect a 40 MPH speed limit going to any fire and 25 MPH speed limit when returning.

In 1960, John F. Kennedy narrowly defeated Richard M. Nixon in the presidential election and became the first Roman Catholic president of the United States and one of the youngest men ever to be elected. "Camelot" had come to the White House bringing with it a feeling of hope. The world was advancing technologically and the U.S. launched the first weather satellite. In April, however, the United States also launched a "spy" plane over Soviet territory. Piloted by Francis Gary Powers, the plane was shot down over the Soviet Union where he was captured and imprisoned. The American people were shocked when the news of the U-2 flight was finally made public.

Stanley Wertheimer
"Starsh"

Fire Police
June, 1959

Commissioner:
1998

The Fire District requested permission to purchase additional land for the Department and in April, a vote was held and the final results were 54 to 3 in favor of the purchase. There were a number of

Chief William Swan Jr.
1960

1961- Assistant Chief Harry Burr with Cub Scout Pack 113

calls in 1960 but perhaps one of the more difficult was the casino fire at Huntington Beach. It began in the kitchen area next to the ice cream parlor on a hot summer night and the flames quickly traveled and fully engulfed the entire casino. Firefighters fought the inferno for several hours and eventually extinguished the flames. Later that same week, a man came into the firehouse and requested a burning permit in order to discard a "small amount of rubbish". The Fire Department

President Bart Heaney
1960-1961

Chief William Kelsey
1961-1962

William Bohaty
"Boom-Pa"
Engine Co. #1
September, 1961
Rescue Squad: 1963 -
Present
Chief: 1978
1st Asst. Chief: 1977-1976
2nd Asst. Chief: 1975-1974
Engine Co. #1:
Captain, Lieutenant
E.M.T.: 1971-1978
Huntington Fire Advisory
Board - Present
Huntington Fire Chiefs'
Countil: Past President

Louis Rispoli
"Louie"
Fire Police
January, 1962
Chief: 1976-1977
1st Asst. Chief: 1974-1975
2nd Asst. Chief: 1972-1973
Benevolent Association:
Past President
Fire Police:
Captain: 1985-1991
Lieutenant: 1984
Hose Company:
Captain: 1967-1969
Lieutenant: 1965-1966
Service Company:
Lieutenant: 1982
E.M.T.: 1972-1977

Bruce M. Jennings

Eagle Truck Co. #1
September, 1962
Rescue Squad: 1963-1996
Captain: 1979-1980, 1995-
1996
Lieutenant: 1975-1978,
1994
Hose Company:
Lieutenant: 1971
A.E.M.T. - Past
PADI certified
1996 Rescue Man of the
Year Award

was once again called to Huntington Beach to fight a fire at the casino. The man, who had requested the permit, had set fire to what remained of the building. There was nothing left of the casino after the second fire.

The Cold War left its mark on the start of 1961 when, on January 3 the President severed America's diplomatic relations with Cuba. Three months later, in April, the Bay of Pigs occurred and Americans held their breath until the crisis passed. Nuclear war was a subject discussed by people all over the United States. In June, Harry Burr and Joe Jaret took a radiological course, which trained them on how to detect radiation with a Geiger counter. Soon after the crisis with Cuba, Alan Bartlett Shepard, Jr., became the first American in space, which took the attention off the Cold War for a little while. People all over the nation were mesmerized as they watched the space mission on television and heard Shepard communicate by radio to ground control from his Mercury space capsule.

Brush fires sprouted up all over Centerport during the summer. Centerport Fire Department worked for four days attempting to put out one such brush fire on Stony Hollow Road but, because of the vast amount of peat moss, it was virtually impossible to stop the fire from spreading. The flames "hid" under the moss and then surfaced sporadically keeping the fire active and dangerous.

The community was growing rapidly and due to the large increase in parishioners in Our Lady Queen of Martyrs Church on Prospect Road, a wing was added to enable the church to hold more people.

On February 20, 1962 the nation once again turned its attention to the skies when Lt. Col. John H. Glenn became the first American to orbit the Earth, circling

the globe three times in his Mercury capsule "Friendship 7". Earlier in the month, on February 7, the Service and Salvage Company was organized to help out the other companies at the scene of a call. At nighttime fires and car accidents, the Service and Salvage Company would set up lights to enable the firefighters and rescue workers to see better. They were also responsible for covering furniture at house fires in order to help protect and save as much property as possible. A deadly fire hit the Ragle household late one March night at the home of the Town Tax Receiver, her daughter, son-in-law and granddaughter. Mrs. Ragle was not home at the time, however the other family members were. Unfortunately, her daughter and a granddaughter did not survive. Mrs. Ragle's granddaughter, however, escaped the fire due to the efforts of her father who threw her to safety as

1962- 25A / Washington Drive on arrival and later

the house burned.

The Spring of 1959 also saw the ground breaking for the new Centerport Postal Office. On September 5, a parade and dedication was held.

In the 1960's many people were traveling by commercial airlines and Long Island residents were constantly reminded of this, as planes routinely flew over their communities. Ninety-five passengers were killed on March 1 when a plane crashed in Jamaica Bay after taking off from Idlewild Airport, today known as Kennedy Airport. On August 20,

President James Armstrong
1962-1963

Chief Harry Burr - 1963

the Grumman Aircraft Corporation invited fire departments from all over the Island to tour the plant and to participate in lectures and demonstrations on firefighting and aircraft crash rescue techniques. The Department participated in this first of many sessions at Grumman. In October, the advanced technology of the United States showed on aerial photos that the Soviets had set up offensive missile bases in Cuba, only 80 miles off the coast of Florida. On October 22, 1962 President Kennedy ordered a blockade on Cuba and gave the Soviet Premier Khruschev an ultimatum. After many days of discussion, the Soviets gave in and dismantled their missile bases. Another collective sigh of relief was heard from the American people.

On March 6, 1963, at the Centerport Yacht Club, two young boys wandered out into the harbor at low tide and became stuck in the mud up to their waists. The boys were discovered as the tide began to come in and the Fire Department was immediately called to rescue the boys. The firefighters and rescue workers were racing Mother Nature to help these trapped children and were successful in their rescue attempt as the boys were brought to safety. One month later, during a test drive in the Atlantic, 129 crewmembers died when the USS Thresher, a nuclear powered submarine, sank.

Problems in Vietnam were heating up and by November there were approximately 15,000 U.S. troops in Vietnam. When Vietnamese President Ngo Dimh Diem was assassinated on November 2, 1963, the power struggle for control of the government began in earnest. On November 22, President John F. Kennedy was assassinated while riding in a motorcade in Dallas. Lee Harvey Oswald, the accused gunman, was taken into custody and, while being escorted to his arraignment,

was shot to death by Jack Ruby in front of the national television audience. The Nation came to a halt as President Kennedy was laid to rest in Arlington. It was a time th Nation will never forget. Even today, people ask the question, "Where were you when President Kennedy was shot?"

In January of 1964 the first reports were released from the Surgeon General of the U.S. that the smoke from cigarettes could kill.

Centerport Front Line in the early 60's

Chief John Kearney
1964-1965

Other health studies expanded on this, and revealed the dangers of inhaling hazardous materials, which warranted the use of protective breathing apparatus for all firefighters. On February 7, the Beatles "invaded" the U.S. when they landed at Kennedy Airport. Music throughout the world would never be the same. Issues in Vietnam worsened when three North Vietnamese PT boats attacked an American destroyer off the Gulf of Tonkin on August 30 and the U.S. retaliated by bombing North Vietnam. That same week, the Gulf of Tonkin Resolution was drawn which granted President Lyndon Johnson extraordinary powers to protect the United States against Southeast Asia.

In the spring, a letter was received from the Huntington Beach Community Association, which concerned the expansion of the Grant Street Firehouse. A larger facility was needed in order to accommodate more equipment. The Commissioners hired an architect to draw plans for the replacement of Station One.

In January, Assistant Chief Kenneth Swan commended the Department for their efforts in trying to save the Comito home on Route 25A. Although the flames destroyed the home, the firemen never gave up and worked hard in their attempt to extinguish the fire. Chief Kearny reported on February 3 that the Huntington Beach Community Association had approved leasing the Grant Street property to the Fire District, which would allow the new substation to be built. On July 6 the contract was signed for the new Firehouse and on November 27, a dedication was held for the new Station One.

President Leroy Jaret
1964-1965

William J. Casey

Fire Police
June, 1965

Hook & Ladder Co.:
Captain: 1974-1975
Engine Co. #1:
Lieutenant: 1973
Rescue Squad: 1972-1978
E.M.T.: Past
1995 Life Saving Award

James M. Feeley
"CJ"

Eagle Truck Co. #1
June, 1965

Rescue Squad: 1971-Present
Chief: 1984-1985
1st Asst. Chief: 1982-1983, 1998
2nd Asst. Chief: 1980-1981, 1996-1997
Engine Co. #3:
Captain & Lieut: 1970 - 1972
Engine Co. #2: Captain: 1973
Hook & Ladder:
Captain & Lieut: 1991-1994
Scuba Squad: Captain: 1988-1989
Huntington Fire Chiefs' Council
President 1984-85
Commissioner: 1988-1990
1992 Fireman of the Year
E.M.T.: 1974-Present
A.E.M.T.:1978-1985

Gus Zeis

Engine Co. #2
December, 1965

Chief: 1992-1993
1st Asst. Chief: 1990-1991
2nd Asst. Chief: 1988-1989
Rescue Squad: Past
Company #2
Captain: 1980-1981
Lieutenant: 1979-1980
Company #3:
Captain: 1972-1973
Lieutenant: 1971, 1978-1979

Paul Stevenson
"Rock"

Engine Co. #2
December, 1966

Commissioner: 1991-Present
Chief: 1988-1989
1st Asst. Chief: 1986-1987
2nd Asst. Chief: 1984-1985
Engine Co. #3:
Captain: 1976-1977, 1983
Lieutenant: 1974-1975

In March, the Department responded to a fire on the corner of 25A and Centershore Road at the Mankin home during a freezing rain storm. The trucks had a hard time with the weather and the Hook and Ladder truck actually slid down the hill and headed towards the Post Office. Luckily, one of the men was able to get in the truck to stop it before it crashed. Unfortunately, however, the house was lost in the fire.

In June, the U.S. conducted the first mass bombing raid in Vietnam and President Johnson increased U.S. troop levels in South Vietnam. At home, the draft quotas were raised to fulfill the President's mandate. The war was affecting the entire nation and not everyone supported it. On October 15 and 16, the first nationwide anti-war demonstration took place and draft cards were burned in protest of the war.

On November 9, a freak power failure blacked out the entire northeast. People were stranded in subways, elevators and office buildings. Some areas were left without power for two days while some areas remained in the dark for up to a week. All police and firefighters were placed on emergency duty similar to the actions that would be taken during a blizzard. The Department members drove around in the Service Truck in order to start up furnaces for the elderly and help families with food and needed supplies.

On January 30, 1966 Geide's Inn, one of the most widely known restaurants on the north shore of Long Island, was destroyed by fire. An employee discovered the fire in the 60 year old structure at 9:45 PM. Luckily, due to a weather forecast, which predicted a snow storm, there were only 12 patrons in the restaurant that night, and all escaped unharmed. More than 200 firefighters from Centerport, Northport, Halesite, Huntington and Greenlawn fought the blaze, which burned for several hours.

Under the direction of Chief Kenneth Swan, the Centerport Fire Department remained at the scene until the late morning to make sure that the fire did not ignite again. Arthur Riedel, the owner of the restaurant, estimated the loss at $750,000 to $1,000,000 and never rebuilt the restaurant.

Geides Inn - Loss of a Landmark
Clippings Courtesy of Jim Varese

This Page Sponsored By:

President William Swan Jr.
1966-1967

1966 - Dedication of the Gong - An old railroad tire

On May 9, the Department attended another Grumman aviation course on fighting aircraft fires. A contract was signed on June 15 with Metropolitan Equipment Corporation for a new Superior ambulance. The ambulance, along with a new Mack 1000 GPM (gallons per minute) pumper, which became Engine 3, were both ready for operation in September.

During the summer, the Cold Spring Harbor Fire Department celebrated its 115th anniversary and Centerport participated in the parade. The weather was great while the departments were lining up for the parade, but once the parade was under way, rain began to fall. As the rain poured down on all the firefighters and spectators, the festivities continued. When the members of the Centerport Fire Department passed the judging table, they quacked like ducks, which showed the spectators that even the rain could not stop them from having a good time.

There were a few "firsts" in 1967. Medical pioneer, Dr. Christian Barnard, performed the first human heart transplant, a relatively common operation today and Sir Francis Chichester, a pioneer in a different field, completed the first solo sail around the world.

On March 20, New York State Law banned the burning of brush and leaves as a Health Department move against air pollution. This ban was enforced by both health and Fire Department officials. In July a fire occurred at the Morrel house off of Little Neck Road. The fire happened on a hot summer night and the huge waterfront house was fully involved when the Department arrived. The fire was throwing embers into

Chief Kenneth Swan
1966-1967

Paul E. Heglund
Engine Co. #2
June, 1968

Chief: 1996-1997
1st Asst. Chief: 1994-1995
2nd Asst. Chief: 1993
Engine Co. #3
Captain: 1975-1976
Lieutenant: 1973-1974
Engine Co. #2
Captain: 1987-1989
Lieutenant: 1985-1986
Scuba Squad:
Lieutenant: 1997
Rescue Squad: 1968-1997
E.M.T. Past
1978 Fireman of the Year
1979 Huntington Chiefs' Council
Valor Award
1984 & 1993 Valor Award

George S. Pribyl
"Steve"

Eagle Truck Co. #1
September, 1968
Rescue Squad: 1972 -
Present
Chief: 1986-1987
1st Asst. Chief: 1984-1985
2nd Asst. Chief: 1982-1983
Scuba: Captain 1992, Lieutenant 1989
Engine Co. #2: Captain 1975-1976
E.M.T.: 1974-1986
A.E.M.T.: 1978-1986
Huntington Fire Chiefs' Council:
President 1987-1988
Secretary 1984-1985 and 1991 - Present
Suffolk County Fire Rescue &
Emergency Service Commission 1990-
Present

the harbor threatening many of the boats moored close by so firefighters were stationed sporadically in the harbor on boats equipped with extinguishers. The fire did not effect any boats and Chief Swan thanked the men for their efforts.

On October 18, Robert J. Bohaty died of a heart attack at his gas station on Centershore Road in Centerport at the age of 67. He was not only the founder of the Long Island Old Car Club and a member of many other community organizations, he was also a past President of the Centerport Fire Department and Captain of the Fire Police Squad. One year later, on October 27, 1968, the Centerport Garden Club and Northport Lions Club dedicated the Mill Pond Park across the street from the post office as the Robert J. Bohaty Memorial Park.

Halloween in 1967 was a surprisingly quiet night for most districts in the township, and the typical instances of teens opening fire hydrants to flood streets and other mischievous acts did not occur. Only one call was recorded in Centerport from dual brush fires that occurred on both sides of Little Neck Road near Mary's Lane. The alarm came in at 12:15 AM and was put out with little trouble.

The Summer Clam Bake
Left - Getting the Clam Pit ready

Chief Kenneth Klerk
1968-1969

In 1967, about 50 members of the Fire Department purchased fire-band radios so they could receive alarms at home from headquarters.

Tensions were high in 1968 due to the assassinations of two prominent national figures. Attorney General of the United States, Robert Kennedy, and civil rights leader Dr. Martin Luther King, Jr. were both killed by assassins, the latter causing riots in many cities, including Washington DC. The country's economy was feeling the effects of inflation and a budget deficit estimated at $20 million, which resulted in Congress passing an income tax surcharge of 10%. That summer, a proposed extension of the main firehouse was discussed. On June 22, the Department celebrated its 70th Anniversary with a dinner held at the Huntington Town House.

In January of 1969, Richard Nixon was inaugurated President of the United States and New York hero, Joe Namath led the New York Jets to their first Super Bowl championship. When New York City elected to forbid city firefighters from also being fire department members in their home communities, both paid and volunteer firefighters joined together to fight the ban. Many Long Island departments had members who were

President Robert Samek
1968

President J. Greg Sullivan
1969-1970

1969 - A fire on Centershore road by Mill Dam road

City firefighters and did not want to lose these valued volunteers. The Volunteer Firefighters Association of America issued a plea to President Nixon to proclaim a National Firefighters' Day, calling for a constitutional Amendment for firefighters' rights, which was granted. New York City eventually gave up the ban.

On February 11, more than 40 volunteers and 10 trucks were on the scene of a fire in a three family home on Centershore Road. The morning fire, which was of undetermined origin, broke out on the first floor and took more than three hours to put out. A neighbor first spotted the fire and alerted the Department. He then ran across the street and with the assistance of another bystander, helped a mother and her three children escape from the second floor of the burning house. After the fire was put out, only the walls were left standing.

Also in February, the F & M Schaefer Brewing Company awarded Ex- Chief Thomas Utter a plaque for "Outstanding Contribution to Duty and Community" for his over 55 years of active volunteer fire service.

The summer of 1969 was very busy with several different historic events taking place. On July 20, U.S. Astronaut Neil Armstrong became the first person to walk on the moon. Once again the nation gathered in front of the television in order to watch and listen to Armstrong and his fellow astronauts Edwin Aldrin, Jr. and Michael Collins. A few weeks later, in August, a different type of record was set at the Woodstock Music Festival, which took place in upstate New York. An estimated 400,000 to 600,000 people attended the first of its kind festival, which was said to embody the spirit of the 60's.

Edwin Seim was named the Department's heroic "Fireman of the Year" and was also presented with a New York City Fire Department citation by Chief Clifford Long and Lt. John A. Luongo for his heroic act at a fire in Brooklyn. Seim had worked for a beverage company and had the same soft drink route in Brooklyn for 24 years. In the fall of 1969, however, he did more than deliver soft drinks. After observing smoke and flames coming from a two-story house in Brooklyn, he stopped his truck and rushed into the smoke filled building. Putting his own safety at risk, he found a child he heard crying and carried the five-year old girl to safety before the fire trucks arrived at the scene.

Chief Douglas Davidson
1970-1971

Thomas P. Feeley

Eagle Truck Co. #1
June, 1970

Scuba Team: 1987-1998,
Captain: 1987-1988, 1990,
1993, 1997
Lieutenant: 1987-1988,

Engine Co. #2:
Captain: 1980-1981
Lieutenant: 1978-1979

President: 1989-1990
1st V.P.: 1987-1988

Peter Hahn

Engine Co.# 2
June, 1971

Sam Jones

Eagle Truck Co. #1
September, 1971

Hook & Ladder Co. 1:
Captain: 1976-1977
1st Lieutenant: 1974-1975
2nd Lieutenant: 1972-1973
President: 1984-1985
1st Vice President: 1983
2nd Vice President: 1982
Asst. Department
Secretary: 1989-1991
Department Secretary: 1992-
1998
Advanced First Aid - Past

On February 8, 1970 a dramatic rescue took place at the Mill Pond. A passing motorist witnessed three children struggling in the icy water and screeched his car to a stop in order to attempt to help them. The sound of the brakes caught the attention of probationary fire-fighters, Randy Jaret and Russell Seim who immediately jumped into the freezing water and waded to the struggling children. The motorist also dashed into the water to help rescue the third child. The Centerport Fire Department awarded Certificates of Valor to the three men, civilian Joseph McBride of Centerport and probationary firefight-ers Randy Jaret and Russell Seim. Jaret and Seim also received the honor of "Fireman of the Year".

In July, a special District meeting was held to resolve the issue of building a two story addition to the firehouse, however, it was not until December that the referendum was approved by a vote of 431 to 60. In September, President Nixon created National Volunteer Firefighters Recognition Week. On November 11, the Benevolent Association was formed through a by-law change. Harry Burr, Edward Brandmaier and Roy Jaret were the original trustees and served three-year terms. The Benevolent Association was established to provide a death benefit to help defray funeral expenses for the families of deceased firefighters.

In addition to the Vietnam War, the United States faced many other problems in 1970. The falling economy had brought about a recession and unemploy-ment was on the rise. Increased civil disobedience was also a concern. Women rallied nationwide to protest discrimina-tion, and anti-war demonstrations were common all over the country. One demonstration, at Kent State University, turned deadly when the National Guard shot four anti-war protesters.

President Kevin Gallagher
1971-1972

In July of 1971, it became obvious that the drug problem in the U.S. had worsened. The government announced a crackdown on drug use and began testing almost all personnel in South Vietnam for heroin use. The Suffolk County Department of Health began discussions with local agencies, including volunteer fire departments, which focused on the formation of a Countywide Emergency Medical Service. At 4 AM August 28, Hurricane Dorrie hit and caused wide spread destruction throughout the area. After the hurricane, the Department's Certificate of Valor was awarded to Fireman G. Weston who risked his life to save the lives and property of residents on Idle Day Drive.

1971- Building the addition

Chief Donald Miller
1972-1973

Drill at Camp Alvernia - remains of the Chalmers House

In 1972, the drug problem worsened once again and centers for the treatment of teenagers with drug and drug related problems were established all over the country. The World Trade Center's Twin Towers were opened in the financial district of New York City and became the tallest buildings in Manhattan.

On September 6, the first Department meeting in the new addition was held and was presided over by President Kevin Gallagher. On November 25, $300.00 was allocated to furnish the museum room in the Firehouse.

On Wednesday, December 27, two men were killed and one other critically injured when an explosion blew out the wall of Jo Jo's Pizzeria on Little Neck Road. The three men were installing a new tile floor in the store as the explosion occurred, when vapors were ignited by a pilot light from the ovens. Six other stores also fell victim to the explosion. First Assistant Chief, Ed Seim, reported that the explosion was felt in the Firehouse approximately 500 feet from the store. More than 70 Centerport firefighters and eight trucks fought the fires for more than two hours before they were brought under control. Six firemen were treated at the scene for smoke inhalation and the Rescue Squad treated two others for lacerations. After the fire, Frank Covello, the operator of Jo Jo's, testified that he had reported a gas leak to LILCO, now known as LIPA, about 4 PM the day before the explosion occurred. As no repair crew arrived to take care of the

William Sullivan
"Sully"

Eagle Truck Co. #1
December, 1972
Truck Company
Captain: 1978-1980
Lieutenant: 1975-1977
Rescue Squad: 1974-1985
E.M.T.: 1976-1985
A.E.M.T.: Past
Past Cadet Advisor
Treasurer: 1998
Assistant Treasurer: 1990-1997

1973 - a new Chiefs car

President Jerome Kubicki
1973

William Reynolds

Engine Co. #1
June, 1974

1st V.P.: 1/86-6/86
Company #2:
Captain: 1982-1983
1st Lieutenant: 1980-1981
2nd Lieutenant: 1978-1979
Rescue Squad: Past
E.M.T.: Past

Skating on the frozen Mill Pond

John Jensen

Eagle Truck Co. #1
June,1974

James M. Cox
"Jim"

Engine Co. #2
June, 1975

Company #3:
Lieutenant: 1986
President: 1980-1981
1st Vice President: 1979
2nd Vice President: 1978
Commissioner: 1992-1996
Rescue Squad: 1977-1983
Huntington Exempt
Firemens' Assn.:
President: 1990

problem, the Long Island Lighting Company agreed to a settlement totaling $825,000 in the death of the two men and the injury of the other.

In 1973, as in the past, skating was a popular sport on the frozen Mill Pond during the winter. In order to make it safer for the public, the Fire Department stationed life rings with attached ropes around the pond. In case a skater fell through the ice, the rings could be used during a rescue. Eventually, however, the Department had to restrict the area skaters could use to the rear of the Firehouse for their safety. On May 19, Fire Policeman Thomas Utter was named "Fire Policeman of the Year" at the New York State Fire Police meeting held at the Rock Hill fire headquarters. In September, Centerport hosted the 3rd Annual Inter-Departmental Drill of the Volunteer Fire Departments in Huntington Township. Several thousand spectators came to view the drill, which was held at Centerport Beach and, out of eight departments, Centerport came in fourth place overall. Some of Centerport's better events included the "Y" Race, in which one hose is split and targets have to be hit, the Ladder Climb, and the Equipment Exchange. Although Centerport placed 1st in the Efficiency

Chief Edwin Seim
1974-1975

Replacement, Cold Spring Harbor's "Young Savages" were the overall winners for the third year in a row.

In 1973, inflation hit a record 8.5 percent while the dollar was devalued and the price of food escalated. To add to these economic woes, an embargo on oil shipped to the U.S. and all other nations supporting Israel made the monetary situation worse. The members of the 11 nation Organization of Arab Petroleum Exporting Countries (OAPEC) orchestrated a shortage of one of the world's most demanded products. Lines at gas stations were ridiculously long, factories were forced to close and, in an attempt to conserve gas, highway speed limits were reduced to 55 MPH.

In 1974, President Nixon resigned from office after the closely watched Watergate crisis. On a brighter note, 1974 marked the year in which 86 year old Thomas Utter celebrated 60 years of active service in the Department. Still fully involved, he recommended that the Department change the color of the lifesavers stationed around the Mill Pond to red. It was felt that the change in color would make it easier to spot and

save a skater in case of an emergency. On July 5, the Centerport Fire Department responded to a mutual aid in Northport. A boat had overturned in the Long Island Sound at the LILCO basin and there were several drowning victims involved.

The Department responded to another mutual aid in Halesite during the summer. The Huntington Crescent Club had a large fire that started in the Caddy Room, which required the efforts of both Departments. By the time Centerport arrived, the building was fully involved and more water than the engines held was needed. Engine 1 began to draft water out of the swimming pool. There were, however, swimmers floating on rafts in the pool, and, unbelievable as it sounds, they refused to get out of the water. This did not stop the firefighters from doing their job and after all the water had been drafted and the

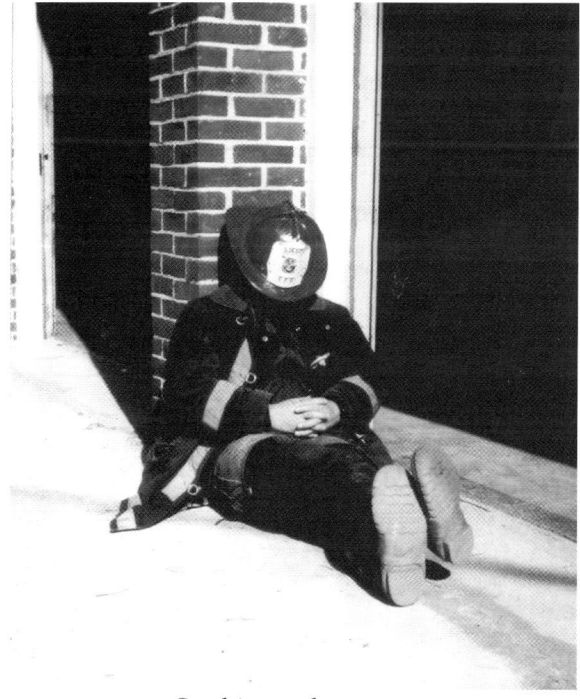

Catching a short nap

This Page Sponsored By:

George & Dorothy Seim

President Patrick Santomauro
1974-1975

fire was put out, the only thing left on the concrete bottom of the pool were the stubborn people on their floats. Ladders from the fire trucks were needed to get them out of the pool.

In August, the first demonstration of Plectron units occurred. The Plectron system would enable all firefighters to hear a call and within minutes, reach their respective stations. It would be a number of years before this system would be in place. On September 15, the Centerport "Sea-Gulls", the Department's drill team, hosted the Annual Huntington Township Drill at Centerport Beach. Also in September, the first Ladies Bucket Tournament in the Town of Huntington was held and the Centerport "She-Gulls", comprised of members of the Ladies Auxiliary, competed.

On December 19, Emergency Medical Technical certificates were awarded to 46 graduates of a course sponsored by the Department. Senior instructor and course coordinator LeRoy Jaret presented the certificates to each student who had successfully completed the course, twenty-three of whom were Centerport firefighters.

On April 30, 1975 the United States pulled out of Vietnam. The last U.S. citizens were airlifted out of South Vietnam thus putting an end to the war. The total amount of fire alarms in 1975 was 142 while the Rescue Squad responded to 299 calls for the year. On February 13, a fire that was caused by a gas space heater gutted a bungalow on Adams Street. The fire broke out at 4:31 PM when no one was at home. It took 42 firefighters about 40 minutes to control the fire, however, seven Centerport fire trucks remained on the scene for two hours.

On March 7, at 2:45 AM, there was a house fire on Washington Drive, which started in a linen closet

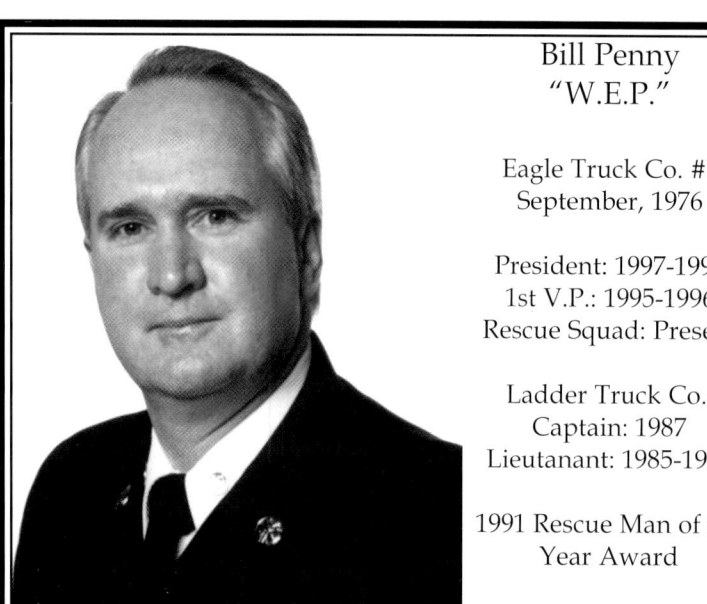

Bill Penny
"W.E.P."

Eagle Truck Co. #1
September, 1976

President: 1997-1998
1st V.P.: 1995-1996
Rescue Squad: Present

Ladder Truck Co.:
Captain: 1987
Lieutanant: 1985-1986

1991 Rescue Man of the
Year Award

on the second floor. Mrs. Kotel was awakened by the smell of smoke and after waking her husband, the two ran through the upstairs hallway, which was filled with smoke and flames, in order to rescue their two daughters. Both parents suffered burns on their feet and smoke inhalation. One daughter was fine, but the other had stopped breathing. A neighbor revived the young girl using mouth to mouth resuscitation after which she was taken to the hospital and treated with the rest of her family. Sixty Centerport firefighters knocked down the flames within in few minutes and six fire trucks remained at the scene until 4 AM.

Edward McGuire

Eagle Truck Co. #1
September, 1976

Commissioner 1994 -
Present

Past Officer:
Service Company
Fire Police

Rescue Squad 1974-1986
EMT: Past

In June all of the nursing homes in the area had smoke detectors and sprinkler systems installed for the increased safety of the residents.

Patrick Fallon was named "Fireman of the Year" and received the Valor Award for his efforts on Little Neck Road during a lightening storm. Lightening had struck a house and the electrical service wire had landed on a chain link fence surrounding the home causing it to become electrically charged, thus preventing the Department from getting to the house. Fallon used his knowledge of electrical equipment to safely remove the wire.

The nation celebrated its bicentennial birthday 1976 in grand style. One of the most exciting events to take place in the New York area was "Operation Sail". Square-rigged sailing ships from all over the world participated in the special event, which was to culminate on July 4th in the New York Harbor. On Friday, July 2, however, some of the ships that were sailing from Newport to New York, put to port in Huntington Harbor. Other events for the big celebration included displays of fireworks and parades throughout the Island and in the City. The Suffolk County Water Authority even agreed to allow the fire hydrants to be decorated with bicentennial themes.

Chief Louis Rispoli
1976-1977

President George Tischner
1976-1977

1976 - Fassade fell off the front of the Little Neck Stores

On May 24, a fire was set to cover up a robbery at the Tryson Lumber Corporation on Fort Hill Road. The fire was fought by more than 180 firefighters from Centerport, Halesite, Greenlawn and Huntington Manor. The blaze was reported at 3:39 PM and by 5:15 PM was under control. The fire sent 14 firemen to Huntington Hospital after polyvinyl chloride pipes inside the lumber-yard began to burn causing toxic fumes to fill the air. The men were treated for inhalation and thankfully released. In June, several storefronts in the shopping area on Little Neck Road collapsed throwing the brick facing off of the buildings into the parking lot. No injuries were reported from the collapse. William Bohaty was installed in June as Vice President of the Huntington Fire Chiefs' Council. The Council, composed of the Chief officers and Ex-Chiefs from the 12 town fire departments continues to meet monthly to solve problems common to all departments in the Town.

A new Mack Quad Pumper was purchased in May at a cost of $86,700 to replace the Hook and Ladder truck. In August the new combination pumper and ladder truck, which contained 172 feet of ground ladders as well as a 1500-gallon per minute pump, was placed into service. A new Hurst Tool, hydraulic jaws used to extricate victims from cars, trucks, and buses that are involved accidents, was also placed into service.

On September 15, the Department's Rescue Squad applied their CPR training to sustain life support functions on a cardiac arrest victim. Arrest occurred in a doctor's waiting room and CPR was commenced within the first minute. The Rescue Squad took over upon their arrival, with Captain Roy Jaret performing chest compressions and EMT David Murphy applying ventilation by use of a regulator. The other crew members, EMT Paul Heglund, AFA Jeffrey Marshall, Paul Rispoli and Richard Jensen gave total support. The many hours they had devoted to training paid off when the

1976 - Tryson Lumber fire

call came from the hospital advising them that the man had survived.

Weather conditions during the winter sometimes pose a challenge to firefighters and rescue workers trying to reach a call, however, the members of the Centerport Fire Department always seem to find a way to get the job done. One such event occurred when a snowstorm had deposited 4 to 6 inches of powder over roads already covered with ice. A call came in from a man who was ill in his home at the top Lone Oak Drive. Due to the poor weather conditions and the steep angle of the street, the man was hand passed on a stretcher over slippery snow from his home to the ambulance by several rescue workers. About 20 firemen then lowered the ambulance containing the man several hundred feet down the steep icy hill via a rope tied around the bumper. Inside the ambulance, Rescue Captain Thomas Lawless, Ex-Captain Patrick Fallon, Bruce Jennings and Conrad Zink gave emergency first aid to the patient while driver James Ryan Jr. carefully maneuvered the ambulance. Over all, 1976 had been a productive year with the Department responding to a total of 519 alarms.

Firefighters Rich Jensen & Paul Stevenson

1977 was a year in which several historic events occurred. The year began with the receipt of a letter from the Harborfields Central School District on gifting the Little Neck School bell to the Department. The Little Neck School was located on the site where the Centerport Methodist Church is currently situated and was always a meaningful part of the history and heritage of the community. After months of discussion, the Little Neck Bell Committee met with representatives of the Department and the Greenlawn-Centerport Historical Society and decided that the Department should display the

Fighting a L.P. gas fire at the Yaphank Training Facility

1976 - Fire at Hunt Country Furniture

school bell as a historical memento of the community. The bell was on the original Centerport School, which later became the Fire Department and, at one time, was used to notify members of the Department of an alarm. Today, the Little Neck School bell is displayed on Park Circle in the front of the Centerport Fire Department with a plaque that reads, "In memory of our firefighters who have answered their last alarm. Their devotion to duty has made Centerport a better community".

Less than a month later, Centerport Fire Department was involved in another historic event. This event, however, had an impact on a community quite distant from Centerport. The "Blizzard of 1977" hit at the peak of the most severe winter to hit Buffalo and the Erie County area in years. In an effort to provide assistance to the snowbound City of Buffalo, then New York Secretary of State, Mario Cuomo urged local fire departments to volunteer equipment and firefighters to assist in the massive clean-up operations. In a mutual aid action unprecedented in the history of the State of New York, six Long Island fire departments were called upon to provide the necessary emergency firefighting equipment. Under the command of Ex-Chief and Chief Deputy Fire Safety Coordinator

Joseph Jaret, six four wheel drive pumpers, and 17 firefighters, who had volunteered their time without pay, were picked up by two U.S.A.F. C-141 cargo planes at the Suffolk County Airport in Westhampton and flown to Buffalo. In an article from a Buffalo newspaper published after all the roads had been plowed, one resident wrote, "In our memory for years to come will be the gracious and timely assistance we received from our Long Island friends and neighbors".

Car fire on 25A - the VW engine

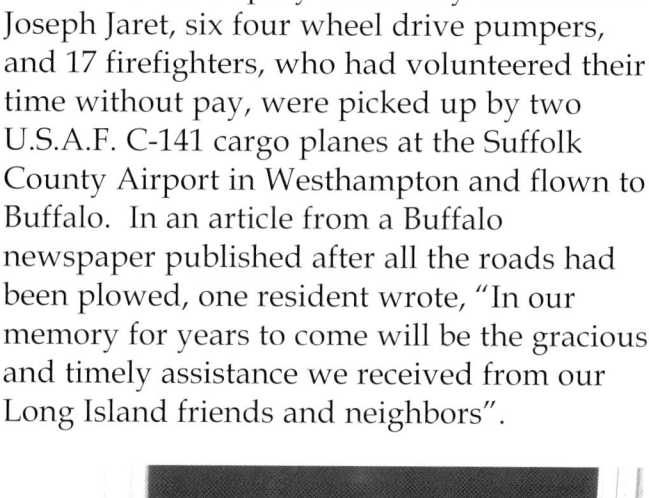

The summer began with a fire on May 31 on Forest Drive. At approximately 4:00 A.M., while the entire family was asleep, a fire broke out in the kitchen. They were fortunate, however, that the family dog was alert and able to awake both parents and their son with her barking. As the family ran to safety, they took the dog and three of her puppies. As Chief Rispoli arrived, heavy fire was visible through the front door and windows and the family told Chief Rispoli that there was still one puppy trapped in the house. As the apparatus arrived, Chief Rispoli ordered the firefighters to make an aggressive attack and to search for the one remaining puppy. Once again, the Department was able to make a "good stop" and within 25 minutes the fire was under control and the puppy was safely returned to her mother and family.

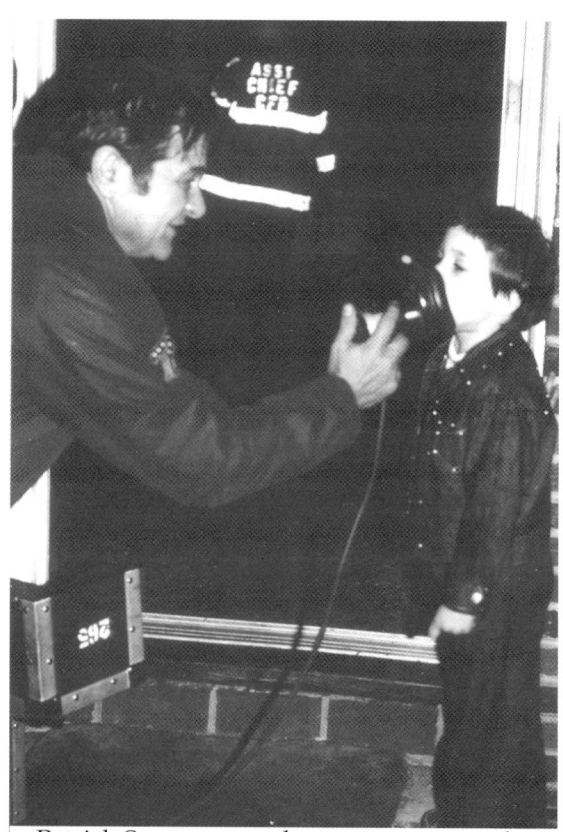

Patrick Santomauro shows a youngster the Oxygen

On Friday morning, June 17, two armed men dressed in masks and gloves robbed the Centerport Post Office, which was a first for the area. The Suffolk County Police gave the following account of the robbery, as reported in the Long Islander: "One man armed with a hand gun walked into the Centerport Post Office around 11:10 A.M. and jumped up on the counter. He ordered the patrons and employees to lie down on the floor and let his accomplice in through the back door. The second man was carrying a shotgun. One of the gunmen ordered the employees to open the two office safes. He then filled two mailbags with about $10,000.00 in stamps, $1,000.00 in post office cash, $1,100.00 in blank postal money orders and a validating machine. When the holdup men first entered the post office there were five employees and only a few patrons, including children. While the one man filled the mailbags, his accomplice hid in the corner of the room and ordered the incoming patrons to lie on the floor. As the gunmen were preparing to leave, they decided to take all of the money the patrons had also. They apologized and said they had to, "do this because we are unemployed." They took about $1,000.00 from the patrons. The robbers left with the mail bags in the Assistant Postmaster's car. As they were leaving the parking lot they hit another car but were able to continue. Assistant Postmaster Walter McKay's car was found by the police later, abandoned on Stony Hollow Road." Neither of the gunmen was ever apprehended and there were never any suspects questioned in the robbery.

1977 was also a year in which the Department and neighboring Northport Fire Department joined together in advancing the technology of each department to better serve their communities. Chief Rispoli arranged for Northport to train with the Department on the new Hurst tool, commonly known as the "Jaws of Life". The Hurst tool is powered by either a gasoline or electric engine,

which pumps hydraulic oil to the tool and can provide up to 15,000 pounds of opening force. Today, as a result of their willingness to explore and train using new technology, the Hurst tool has enabled both departments to rescue victims from a motor vehicle accident in seconds. Currently, the Department carries three such Hurst tool devices that allows the Department to perform patient care as quickly as possible. In some instances, this means the difference between life and death.

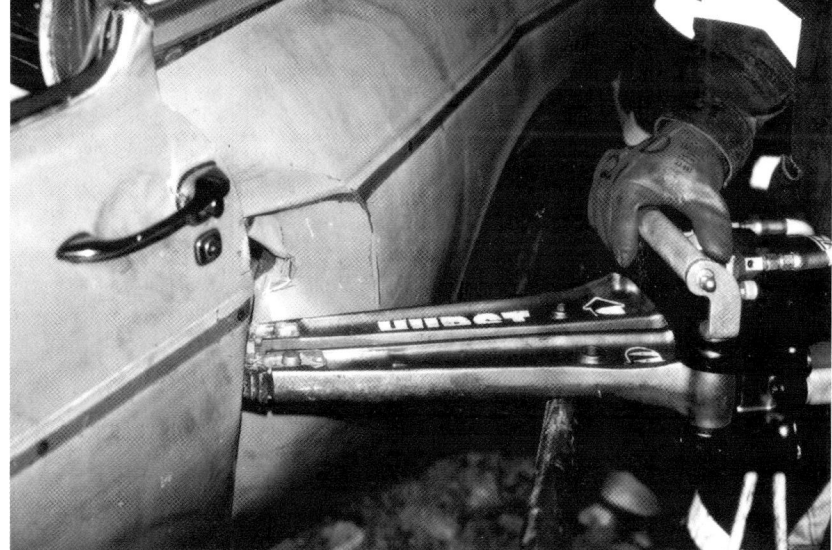

Another innovative joint venture for both departments was the implementation of the Plectron radio system, first demonstrated in 1974. At the time, when an alarm was activated, the Department would utilize the sirens and a special telephone system to notify the firefighters. The phone system used special phones in firefighters' homes, which the firefighter would have to answer in order to learn where the call was located. The phone system was costly,

Chief William Bohaty
1978

President Edward Hallenback
1978

and the Department often encountered difficulty in hooking the units up in the firefighters' homes and/or places of business. The sirens were of limited effectiveness because if firefighters were unable to hear the sirens, they were unaware that an emergency existed. With the one-way Plectron radios, firefighters would be informed of the location of an alarm in any location because Plectron radios connected to any electrical outlet and therefore could be transported with the firefighter. As a result of the new Plectron system, both Centerport and Northport created a "back-up" system to give both departments the ability to activate the other department's system in case of an emergency. Currently, the "back-up" system is still in effect for both departments, as well as the Eaton's Neck Fire Department.

In continuing its efforts to better serve the Centerport community, the Department placed a new Yankee Coach Modular Ambulance into service during mid-1977. Soon after, to the delight and excitement of the Department and Centerport community, the Department's Rescue Squad became one of the first New York State-Certified Fire Department Ambulances on Long Island. Both the new modular ambulance and the old Cadillac ambulance had to meet stringent requirements set by the State Board of Health in order to qualify and were required to carry an extensive amount of emergency equipment. One piece of equipment that enabled the ambulance to become a primary advanced life support vehicle was the addition of the telemetry EKG unit which allows firefighters to determine a patients heart rhythm, which aids in treating a cardiac patient. Other factors that determined the Department's eligibility for certification were the Rescue Squad members' levels of training and the requirement that there be at least one Emergency Medical Technician (EMT) on every ambulance call. At the time, the Department's Rescue Squad, led by Captain Lewis Scarduzio, had a total of 43 members, including 32 who were EMT qualified and 6 who had earned the higher Advanced EMT qualification.

1977 ended with the official opening of the newly reconstructed Mill Dam Causeway on December 2. In addition to providing a safer, more scenic bridge, a fishing bulkhead was also constructed for use by the Centerport residents.

William Bohaty was Chief and Edwin Hallenback became President in 1978 as the Department celebrated

James Reilly

Engine Co. #2
March, 1978

Benevolent Assn.
President/Trustee: 1996-1998

President: 1986-1987
1st Vice President: 1984-1985
2nd Vice President: 1983

1992 Valor Award

Bill Bokelmann
"Bill"

Engine Co. #1
June, 1978
Commissioner: 1994-Present
Rescue Squad: 1990 -Present

Engine Co. #1:
Captain: 1995
Lieutenant: 1994
C.P.R.
1989 Act of Valor Award

80 years of dedicated service. It wasn't long before the Department was put to work under the command of Chief Bohaty. On Friday, January 13th, Long Island was hit with its second big ice storm in three years. Huntington Township was hit the worst on Long Island with power lines dangling through trees and across the roads. Trees also blocked many of the Town's roads, making it difficult, if not impossible, for many people to get home from work and icy road conditions made it exceedingly hazardous to travel. Power went off in Centerport permanently at about 11:00 P.M., Friday night and, for many people, did not come back on until the following Wednesday night. At 12:30 A.M., Saturday morning, Chief Bohaty alerted a stand-by for both the Main House and Station One. As soon as the firefighters arrived at their respective stations, they were immediately dispatched on calls for wires down, fallen trees on wires and trees blocking roads. Apparatus rolled throughout the Centerport area, clearing roads and securing fallen wires. Although the Department was not responsible to clear fallen trees in the roadway, Chief Bohaty ordered that all trees be cleared so the apparatus would have a clear path in case of a fire or other emergency.

Chief Bohaty extended the stand-by to cover Saturday night and most of the firefighters left their families for a second straight night so that they could give their time at the Firehouse. Some of the firefighters brought their families with them and other Centerport residents fled their cold homes to spend some warm nights at the Firehouse. People brought the food that they had in their freezers and everybody had a good hot meal. The Department supplied cots and blankets along with food. Firefighters continued to go out on some alarms Saturday night, again fighting severe weather conditions. On Sunday night, Chief Bohaty called off the mandatory stand-by and the Department looked forward to a well-deserved rest. The rest, however, did not last long as the firefighters were called out for two house fires, on Centershore Road and Lone Oak Drive. Fortunately, both fires

This Page Sponsored By:

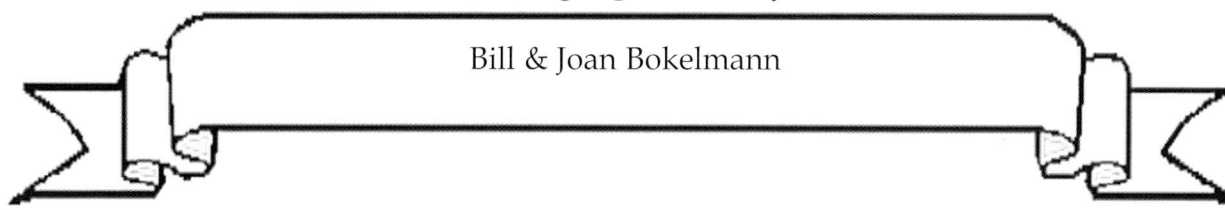

Bill & Joan Bokelmann

Thomas Boyd
"Floyd"

Eagle Truck Co. #1
September, 1978

Ladder Co. #1:
Captain: 1986-1987, 1990
Lieutenant: 1984-1985,
1989

E.M.T.: 1979 - 1981
Rescue Squad: 1978 - 1981
PADI Certified Diver

John Malico

Engine Co. #1
December, 1978

Engine Co. #2:
Captain: 1986
Lieutenant: 1984-1985

Rescue Squad: 1979- 1992
Advanced First Aid - Past

were minor, and, for the second time in under a year, the family dog alerted the household that there was a fire and all were able to escape without injury.

Just as things were starting to look brighter with power restored and streets cleared, Long Island was hit on Thursday, January 19 with the worst snowstorm since 1969. Power went out again, and Chief Bohaty called the firefighters early Friday morning for another stand-by. This time, the firefighters remained on stand-by for approximately 14 hours before being released late Friday evening. In all, it had been a very busy and hectic week for both the Department and residents of the Centerport community.

In contrast to the hard winter, the remainder of the year saw more positive events unfold. In June, the Department and Centerport resident Warren Newman completed the restoration of the hand pumper. The hand pumper was originally

The Ice storm forces people out of their homes

built in 1886 and was purchased by the Department in 1899 for $600.00. After its much-anticipated restoration, the hand pumper went on to win many awards including the award for best restored hand pumper at Valhalla, New York. Then, on September 6, the Department had another reason to celebrate when the Rescue Squad placed its first Advanced Life Support, or ALS, unit in operation.

After a Hurst tool drill

Ex-Chief Thomas Utter became the sixth recipient of the prestigious Fire News Lifesaver's Cup. The trophy, intended to honor all senior members of the volunteer fire service, is awarded yearly and housed in the recipient's Department. Ex-Chief Utter had given a lifetime of public and Department service to the Centerport community and, after 60 years of service, was still active at the age of 90. Ex-Chief Utter is a prime example of the type of dedication on which the Department prides itself.

As the finale of the 80th Anniversary Celebration, the members of the Department decided to build a time capsule. Memorabilia was collected and sealed in a capsule and placed in a monument in front of the main Firehouse on Park Circle. Included in the capsule were the minutes of the Department's October 1978 meeting which include details of the capsule and instructions to open the monument in 2048 when the Department will celebrate its 150th Anniversary. There were also several messages and greetings to the future Chief and firefighters of the Department, as well as a check for $1.00 payable November 1, 2048. Other items placed in the capsule included the program from the 80th Anniversary Dinner signed by all the members at the dinner, a copy of Fire News, and several items donated by Centerport residents.

William Wamp II became Chief and Edwin Seim became President in 1979 and, just as it was for his predecessor, it did not take long before Chief Wamp was put to work. On January 6, with the roads icy due to another cold winter, a 3,000 gallon oil tanker overturned on Centerport Road near Blenheim Lane and spilled over 250 gallons of oil down Centerport Road toward Route 25A. Chief Wamp and 50 firefighters used a mixture of "light water" foam and water to break down and wash away the oil slick while both the Town of Huntington and Suffolk County Highway Departments responded with sand trucks to help shore up the oil spill. The Department soon discovered that this type of accident would unfortunately not be uncommon in Centerport. In May, another heating oil truck overturned, this time on Route 25A, and spilled hundreds of gallons of fuel.

In 1979, the historic Little Neck School, which had given its bell to the Department in 1977 and was a part of the history and heritage of the Centerport community, was sold to the Centerport Methodist Church. Ex-Chief Thomas Utter became the first Department member to receive the honor of "Chief Emeritus". Only an Ex-Chief who obtains 40 years of active service may qualify for this designation which is given by the Chief of the Department. This was quite an honor for a very deserving man.

In May, the Department implemented a new Suffolk County program for its senior population. A "vial for life" container was offered free of charge to residents aged 60 and over. The vials, which were the size of a cigar tube and made of plastic, were promoted and recognized nationally as an

President Edwin Seim
1979

Chief William Wamp Jr.
1979, 1981

instrument in which to store an individual's medical history and medication needs. They were designed to fasten to the top shelf of a refrigerator, as every home has one and they tend to survive catastrophic events. Refrigerator decals were also made available to indicate the presence of the vials.

In June, a bill sponsored by Assemblyman John J. Flanagan was passed by both houses of the State Legislature, which guaranteed, for the first time, the availability of malpractice insurance for volunteer ambulance units which provide Advanced Life Support (ALS). This had a significant impact because the Department had been providing ALS service without insurance and the new legislation made adequate protection available for the many Department members who freely gave of their time and skills to save lives.

Another gas crisis hit during the summer as many local fire departments felt the pinch of a different type of crisis, which involved manpower. For the first time in a decade, many Long Island fire departments, including Centerport, were having trouble not only recruiting new members but also keeping the members they had. Some departments reported difficulty in adequately manning fires during the day and in staffing emergency ambulances. With the tightening economy, many members were forced to get second jobs, go back to school to qualify for higher paying jobs, or move to other areas of the country with lower costs of living. These factors coupled with increased training requirements and alarms, and social pressures to spend more time at home created a decline in the membership of many fire departments. The Long Island fire service was feeling the effect of the changing times.

In the midst of this crisis, the Department went through another change, which would mirror a change in the country as a whole. In 1979, Marilyn Mendez became the first female firefighter to be sworn into the Department. For the first time in the Department's history, the term "fireman" could no longer be used. "Firefighter" would soon become the necessary term to describe the members. Today, the Department is proud to have five female members and several more in the cadet program. Female firefighters have become a part of the fire service around the nation, and a trend, which represents the future of the volunteer fire service.

Richard T. Somma
"Rich Babe"

Eagle Truck Co. #1
June, 1979

Rescue Squad: 1979 - Present

Hook & Ladder Co.:
Captain: 1983-1984
Lieutenant: 1981-1980

E.M.T.: 1979-1989

Regardless of a firefighter's gender, however, the dangers experienced by firefighters remain the same.

Incidents involving arson had been increasing nationwide since the 1950's and by 1979, arson was being viewed as an epidemic. Suffolk County was well equipped to handle this increase, as they provided more manpower and equipment per square mile than any other place in the world. However, as the population of Suffolk County, as well as Centerport expanded, firefighters were faced with a growing number and types of fires. Meanwhile, demands on fire departments for ambulance service also grew, which put most departments more in the business of rescue than firefighting. With a rise in the amount of alarms fire departments were handling on a daily basis, firefighting became an increasingly dangerous job. In less than three years, 11 Long Island firefighters had died in the line of duty.

Tommy Utter shares a story

The local area was suffering from the same fire epidemic as the rest of the Long Island. During the winter of 1979, Chief Wamp and the Department responded to a series of fires within Centerport, including two severe fires in February. Shortly before midnight a fire started on Hayes Place and within days another fire occurred on Upper Pond Court.

Later in the year, the Department assisted the Northport Fire Department with one of the worst fires in Northport's history. On April 30, the Axinn and Sons Lumber Company, located where the King Kullen Shopping Center is now, was completely destroyed by flames. Centerport was there from the beginning to assist Northport. Eventually, however, every fire Department from the Town of Huntington was needed. All 12 departments fought the fire through the night and well into the next morning. Just 10 days later, on May 11, the Department was again called to assist Northport on another lumber yard fire, this one across the street from Axinn's Mill. The Northport Lumber Corporation's storage shed was completely destroyed by the blaze, however, due to the extraordinary efforts of the firefighters, the lumber yard was able to open for business the next day.

The Department continued to have a busy year with an increased amount of fire and rescue alarms.

Centerport assists Northport at the Axinn & Northport Lumbar fires

1979 concluded with a mid-day house fire on Prospect Road on December 15. The efforts of the Department were best described by the owners in a letter published in the December 26, 1979 Pennysaver which read, "On December 15, the Centerport Fire Department saved our home from almost sure total destruction. We do not know of a higher compliment to pay them. We thank God for their immediate response and setup, for their professionalism in entering the burning house despite the intense heat and smoke, and for the absolute care they exercised in preventing further damage to the remaining contents. The Johnson Family is most grateful to the fine group."

John Milligan

Engine Co. #1
December, 1979

Louis Scarduzio became Chief and James Cox was President in 1980, a year in which the New York Islanders won the first of four Stanley Cups and local resident Jerry Cooney was the leading heavyweight contender in the boxing world. CNN became the first 24-hour news television station, and Centerport's historic Linck's Log Cabin went bankrupt. There was also a new awareness of firefighters' safety when the Occupational Safety Hazard Association (OSHA), a federal agency, began to control the fire service and implemented strict guidelines in an effort to increase safety at the scene of an alarm and also at the Firehouse.

The nation found itself in a military crisis in the Middle East with Iran following the takeover of the U.S. Embassy in Tehran. At the January Department meeting, when President Cox called for "new

This Page Sponsored By:

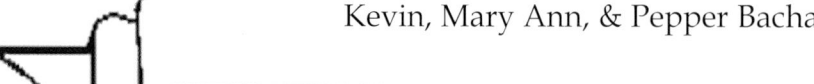

Chief Louis Scarduzio
1980

President James Cox
1980-1981

business" Lieutenant Ed McGuire suggested that the Department should do something to recognize the 52 Americans held hostage in Iran by flying a flag in front of the Firehouse on Park Circle until the hostages were set free. Ex-Chief Lou Rispoli further suggested that bumper stickers be printed so that the sentiments of the Department would be known throughout the Island. A white flag with the number 52 in red was ordered and every member received and displayed their bumper stickers. Residents of the Centerport community were entitled to receive any additional bumper stickers in surplus and the symbolic flag was flown day and night under the United States flag on Park Circle.

Two of the Department's members were honored in February for their heroic efforts in saving the life of another. Ex-Captain Paul Heglund and firefighter James Reilly were on vacation in June 1979 when they rescued a drowning victim trapped underneath an over-turned canoe in the Delaware River. Heglund and Reilly brought the victim to the shoreline and success-fully revived the man using CPR. In recognition of their extraordinary efforts, Heglund and Reilly were awarded the Department's Valor Award and the Life Saving Award from the Town of Huntington Chief's Council.

Later that month the Department was summoned to save the life of one of its residents. On Saturday, February 16, shortly before midnight, two men were driving on Buchanan Street when they noticed smoke billowing from the home. They immediately notified the Department and under the command of Chief Scarduzio, the Department fought a stubborn fire in the kitchen and living room of the two-story home. As the Department was successfully attacking the blaze, Chief Scarduzio received reports that an elderly woman lived in the home and was possibly still inside. The Department took immediate steps to locate and rescue the woman, who was reported to suffer from failing eyesight. Due to the intense heat and smoke, however, the Department was unable to rescue the woman. The Suffolk County Arson Squad later determined that the fire originated in the kitchen. The Department desperately fought the blaze for more than an hour before the fire was brought under control and Chief Scarduzio praised the members for their efforts in trying to save the woman.

Top Left - Free the hostages bumper sticker
Above - A fire on Greenlawn Road - on arrival
Left - The Centerport Drill team

Later that year, the Department honored two Centerport youths who had gone beyond the call of duty to save the life of another with the "Civilian Certificate of Valor" issued by the Board of Fire Commissioners. The award was given in recognition of their selfless action in the rescue of a member's wife who fell through the ice behind the Firehouse on the Mill Pond. The Department later transported the woman, suffering from back pain and a slight case of hypothermia, to Huntington Hospital. Chief Scarduzio indicated that had it not been for the quick action of the two young residents, the woman might not have survived.

After a relatively quiet ending to 1980, things began in 1981 much as it did a year earlier. Chief William Wamp II was again nominated as Chief of the Department after Ex-Chief Scarduzio could only complete one year as Chief. The Department paid tribute to the freed American hostages, as bitter cold winds swirled outside the Firehouse on Park Circle. It was January 29th and the day was declared a day of thanksgiving for their return and also to remember the eight men of our armed services who died in the futile attempt to free them. With yellow ribbons festooning the Firehouse and pinned to winter coats, 92 members stood in sub-freezing weather beside Marines, politicians, Boy Scouts, Girl Scouts and a score of local Centerport residents. They came to watch a ceremony that honored the hostages and the 444 days they remained in captivity. At 8:00 P.M. "Taps" was played and the flag, which had

"52" Hostage flag

Jack W. Geffken, D.O.
"Doc"

Eagle Truck Co. #1
September, 1981
Deputy Chief: 1992 - Present
2nd V.P.: 1997-1998
Rescue Squad: 1982 - Present
Captain: 1986-1987
Lieutenant: 1985
Open Water Diver
Physician
A.E.M.T./E.M.T.: Past
1993 Rescue Man of the Year
1997 Suffolk County E.M.S.
Physician Excellance Award
Originated first diver certifica-
tion course 1986
Suffolk County Medical Control
Field Physician

Robert Simpson
"Bob"

Engine Co. #1
September, 1981
Chief: 1998 - Present
1st Asst. Chief: 1996-1997
2nd Asst. Chief: 1994-1995
Rescue Squad: 1982 -
Present
Engine Co. #1:
Captain 1988-1989
Lientenant 1987-1986
E.M.T.: Past
1990 Firefighter Service
Award (Dedicated Service)

been displayed for over a year, was finally lowered and removed from the Firehouse flagpole. Later, as the enthusiastic crowd gathered to celebrate, Chief Wamp and President Cox led the crowd in signing "God Bless America". After the ceremony, the crowd sought the warmth of the Firehouse for refreshments and to sign the flag in commemoration of the event. From that day on, the flag has been displayed in the Department's museum for all to see.

1981 saw a major transition for the Department, as well as the youth of the Centerport community. In March, the Centerport Fire Department Cadet Training Program was inacted in an effort to alleviate the manpower problems that were threatening the future strength of the Department. It was decided to try to get the youth of the community involved so that in the future, there would be competent fire-fighters ready to be active at age 17. The Cadets, all of whom were between 14 and 17 years old, had to obtain parental permission before they could enter the training program.

Cadets were instructed in standard and advanced first aid and became certified in CPR techniques as well. The most exciting part of the training cycle for the Cadets was dealing with firematics, which included lessons in search and rescue, firefighting methodology and lessons in how to recognize the various stages of a fire. The Cadets were not allowed to participate in a real fire, but the controlled drill exercises were close enough to the real thing. The Cadets also received instruction in how to deal with car and house fires, as well as about basic strategy and equipment intrinsic to firefighting. The Cadet program was headed by Cadet Instructor Andy Mark and the 12 charter members were Andrew Case, Jeff DeCarlo, James DeSantis, Edward Fallon, Patrick Fallon, Mario Gallusio, Matthew Gaurino, Heidi Lewis, Curtis Pyke, Robert Smith, Bill Sullivan, and Oliver Witting. The Cadet program has continued to grow and today there are currently over fifteen boys and girls from ages 13 to 18 who make up the Cadet Training Program.

This Page Sponsored By:

Ryan & Shawn Geffken

Later that summer, Centerport suffered the loss of one of its historic landmarks. On August 26, a little over a year and one-half after it had closed, Linck's Log Cabin was completely destroyed by fire. Linck's was a "famous" family restaurant that had served the Centerport community for more than 53 years before it was closed in January of 1980. People from all over used to eat at Linck's to enjoy its great atmosphere and "good, hearty food at a reasonable price". The fire, which was the second serious fire in the building's history, started at approximately 1:35 P.M. A passing motorist notified the Fire Department that smoke was billowing across 25A from the restaurant. When the firefighters arrived, heavy smoke and fire were visible from the road and within minutes the fire had broken through the roof. Chief Wamp immediately summoned mutual aid from the Greenlawn Fire Department for the use of their snorkel truck. As the inferno began to rage out of control due to the heavy fire load in the abandoned restaurant, additional apparatus and manpower was desperately needed. Firefighters from Greenlawn, Northport, Halesite, Huntington and Cold Spring Harbor were called to the scene to assist in controlling the blaze. A total of 15 pieces of apparatus and 120 firefighters fought the blaze for five and one-half hours before it was brought under control. The Suffolk County Arson Squad determined that the fire, started in a second floor office area, was the result of arson. No one was ever apprehended in connection with the fire and to this date, rumors still surface on how the blaze started. When asked how he believed the fire started, Chief Wamp responded, "It certainly wasn't smoking in bed."

Linck's Log Cabin Fire

Patrick Fallon became Chief and Walter Nass was President of the Department in 1982. New York State enacted its new minimum age drinking law, raising the age from 18 to 21 to become effective in one-year increments over a three-year period. As a result, Chief Fallon reconstructed the Department's drinking guidelines appropriately and no one under 19 was permitted to consume alcohol at Department functions.

Reports reveal that more than 3,000 people die annually in fires around the United States. In addition, more than 15,000 people are injured in fires or by fire related causes each year. In New York alone, over 100 people die and over 1,000 are injured annually in fire related incidences. Over 75% of those deaths and injuries are the result of fires in the home. Safety experts agree that the reason for the high percentage is that people are uneducated with respect to fires. As a result, Operation EDITH, Exit Drill In The Home, was organized to teach students and their families how to escape from their home in case of a fire. Operation EDITH utilizes the joint efforts of the school system and local fire departments to educate students on fire prevention and fire safety.

President Walter Nass
1982-1983

Parents receive letters promoting the beginning of the program each year and the entire family is encouraged to participate in the program. During Operation EDITH, the Department sponsors different events at each school within the Harborfields School District to increase the public's awareness of fire hazards and develop their preparedness for home emergency situations.

In 1982, fully believing that fire prevention is a full time job, Centerport launched a fire prevention program which lasted several months. The schedule began in the middle of August with visits to the Vanderbilt Museum on Little Neck Road. Due to the many irreplaceable and priceless items in the museum, Chief Fallon believed the fire attack plans had to be updated. As part of the Department's continuing fire prevention program, a safety seminar for the employees of the Adult Care Homes in the area was also conducted in late August. Centerport firefighters trained employees of the Mill Pond Manor, Green Tree Manor, Country Lake, Hilltop and Echo Adult Homes on basic fire prevention and fire extinguishing skills. During September, members of the Department visited and worked with teachers in order to stress the importance of fire prevention. In early October, students were invited to participate in the annual poster-essay contest, which stressed fire safety.

The culmination of the first phase of the fire prevention program took place on Sunday, October 10, with an open house and fire prevention demonstration for the entire Centerport community. On October 15, the entire Centerport community joined the Department by participating in Operation EDITH. Phase two of the program concluded in late 1982 with a Christmas fire safety program and a demonstration of ice rescue equipment and techniques. It is these types of programs which illustrate the Department's concern for its community and which set it as one of the leading fire departments in fire prevention. This is also why Centerport is considered one of the safest communities to live in.

Chief Patrick Fallon
1982-1983

The quality of the firefighters is another reason why Centerport has such a good reputation for fire protection. A prime example of that high caliber of firefighter occurred during a fire in August in which one Department member was recognized for his selfless act of bravery in saving the life of a fire victim.

David R. Mc Govern

Engine Co. #1
March, 1982

Assistant Cadet Advisor:
1998
President: 1988
1st Vice President: 1987
2nd Vice President: 1986

Engine Co. #1:
Captain: 1994-1996
Lieutenant: 1992-1993

Ex-Captain Paul Heglund, a recipient of the Department's Valor Award in 1980, was awarded the Thomas F. Dougherty Medal for bravery by the Fire Department of the City of New York (F.D.N.Y.). Paul, who is also a paid firefighter with F.D.N.Y., was at work on August 21 with Ladder Company 38 when a report of a fire with victims trapped was transmitted. The following account is taken from a F.D.N.Y. publication: "On the fourth floor, Paul inched his way across the landing. The rear apartment was a mass of flame. There was no way in. Then he found another door in between the fire apartment and the one entered, but it was locked. Conditions were rapidly deteriorating in the hall, Paul knew he couldn't stay any longer. With a Herculean effort, he forced the door by himself, however, in working his way through, the door lost its integrity and couldn't be closed again. As he tried, fire entered the apartment, now there was no way back. Flames streaking across the ceiling drove Paul to his knees as he crawled on to continue his search for life. Thirty feet into the apartment he found a 35 year old woman, hysterical, unable to scream any longer because of the dense smoke, she frantically clutched at Paul's Scott air mask, so he gave it up to her. Looking out the window, Heglund could see red, yellow and orange flames leaping through the swirling smoke below. Seemingly out of options, Paul radioed for the aerial ladder ...... Heglund was driven back from the window by the intense heat and couldn't see the help on the way. Back in the

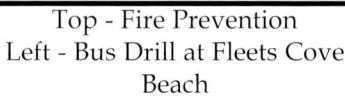

Top - Fire Prevention
Left - Bus Drill at Fleets Cove Beach

Robert Bohaty

Eagle Truck Co. #1
December 1982

Kevin Dearie

Eagle Truck Co. #1
March, 1983
2nd Asst. Chief : 1998
Rescue Squad: 1983 -
Present
Captain: 1988, 1990-1991
Lieutenant: 1986-1987, 1989
Scuba Squad: 1988 - Present
Eagle Truck Co.:
Captain: 1994 - 1995
Lieutenant: 1992-1993
E.M.T.: 1984 - Present
A.E.M.T.: 1997 - Present
1996 Rescue Squad Man of the
Year Award

Thomas G. Liebler
"Llama"

Engine Co. #1
March, 1983

room the woman was frantic.......It (the aerial) arrived on the scene just as he got the woman to the window......Paul returned to his company and continued to operate until the unit was relieved."

It was the Department's 85th Anniversary and a time for celebration, however, 1983 started off on a controversial note. The Harborfields Central School District, under the leadership of Superintendent Spendley, announced that a decision to realign Central School District 6 had been made, and, as a result, the Washington Drive Elementary School would be closed. Many heated public meetings were held and protesters marched in front of the school to display their disapproval of the plan. On February 2, more than 200 Centerport residents, divided by their opinions, appeared at the School Board's session. Things became very heated and several rambunctious members of the audience heckled those who opposed them. Ex-Captain Paul Stevenson expressed the Department's unanimous opposition to the closing of the school and cited the Department's long association with the students and faculty in regard to fire safety. He urged careful consideration of maintaining the neighborhood school, however, the decision to close the school was made. Now it was time to reunite a community that had been so bitterly torn apart.

Just as things started to settle down, another decision once again sparked turmoil within the community. The Centerport Fire District had been in a dispute with the Suffolk County Water Authority for nine years over the ever increasing cost of renting fire hydrants. The fight was lost, however, when a ruling by the New York State Court of Appeals ordered the District to pay Suffolk Water $318,000.00, which included $128,000.00 in back rent for 189 fire hydrants and $190,000.00 in late charges.

Training at the Smokehouse

The water authority had sued the District in order to collect payments that the District had withheld in an attempt to get the authority to negotiate a contract. The decision by the Court also had a significant impact on other fire districts around the state, which also withheld paying the increased fees pending the outcome of the authority's dispute with the District. The dispute with the water authority never interfered with the Department's firefighting capabilities and the Department continued to serve the community as it had for eighty-five years.

In June, Governor Mario Cuomo signed a bill, which would make distinctive license plates available to all volunteer firefighters in New York State. The plates, which were distributed in April 1984, displayed a Maltese Cross and the letters "V" and "F". Every volunteer firefighter would be entitled to one license plate so they could proudly display their membership in their local fire department.

At a year-end celebration of the Department's 85th Anniversary, Ex-Chief George Simpson received a special salute. After completing fifty years of active and distinguished service to the Centerport community, he was given the status of "Chief Emeritus", an honor given to only one other Department member. Ex-Chief Simpson had held many firematic positions including Chief of the Department in 1947 and 1948 and was instrumental in organizing the Rescue Squad, which had grown into an invaluable service for the Centerport community. Many other honors were given to Ex-Chief Simpson not the least of which were letters of congratulation from President Ronald Reagan and Governor Cuomo.

In 1984, James Feeley became Chief of the Department with Sam Jones as President and it wasn't long before the Department was put to work battling a blaze, which would claim yet another well-known Centerport restaurant. It was bitterly cold on Sunday, February 26 and while most of the community was fast asleep the alarm sounded and the members were activated for a report of heavy smoke in the area of the Original Schooner restaurant on Route 25A. As Chief Feeley turned the bend by the Firehouse he was faced with a wall of thick, dense smoke which covered 25A and the Original Schooner and reported that he had a "working fire". As the apparatus arrived members encountered heavy fire erupting through the second and third floors of the restaurant. Chief Feeley immediately requested assistance from the Greenlawn and Northport Fire Departments. Firefighters fought fierce winds and sub-freezing weather as they aggressively attacked the blaze. It was so cold that firefighters had ice hanging from their helmets, coats, and beards and 25A became a sheet of ice. It was hours before the 110 firefighters were able to bring the

Chief James Feeley
1984-1985

President Samuel Jones
1984-1985

blaze under control. Upon investigation, it appeared that the fire originated in the kitchen area after the restaurant had closed. Three firefighters received minor injuries in the Schooner blaze.

March arrived and the Department and Centerport community was once again faced with a controversy. It started with a dispute between the local civic associations and the Department over the proposed

The Schooner Fire

construction of a road to connect Little Neck Road and Prospect Road in the area of the Mill Pond Bridge. The Department and other pro-road representatives urged that the road was a needed emergency access route off the peninsula and would also serve to relieve traffic congestion due to the numbers of visitors who visit the Vanderbilt Museum and Centerport Beach. The civic associations argued that the road would have a significant negative impact on the environment, so, after a long debate, it was decided that the road would not be

Andrew Case
"Andy"

Eagle Truck Co. #1
March, 1984

Eagle Truck Co. #1:
Captain: 1996-1997
Lieutenant: 1994-1995

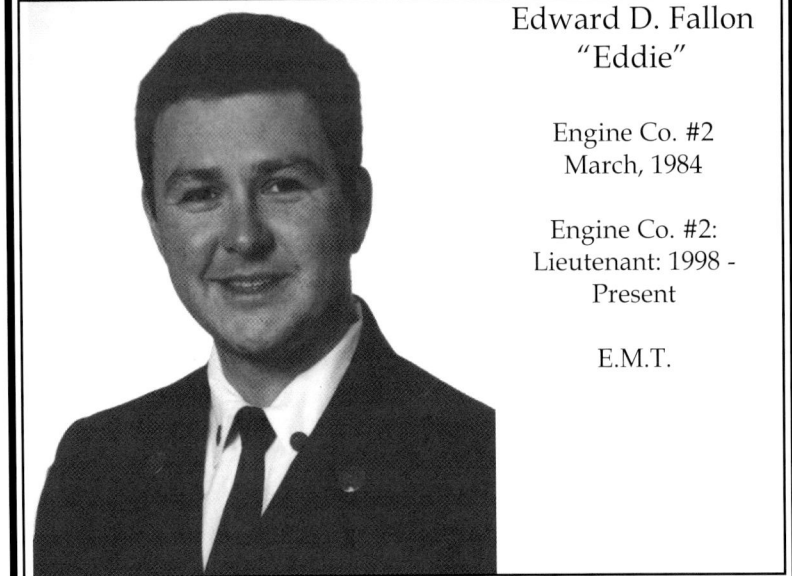

Edward D. Fallon
"Eddie"

Engine Co. #2
March, 1984

Engine Co. #2:
Lieutenant: 1998 -
Present

E.M.T.

constructed. In the past there were two roads that connected the end of Prospect Road to Little Neck. These disappeared in the early 1900's, as did other roads, which can be seen on the 1910 map within this book.

A week or so later, it was rumored that Vengroff, Weiss and Aycock, a local developer, planned to bring house barges into Centerport Harbor. Vengroff, Weiss and Aycock owned a computer software company and the bar Drifter's Reef, both located at the intersection of Mill Dam Bridge and Centershore Road. The developer considered docking four or five house barges in Centerport Harbor near the boat yard they also owned. Although the Town searched for an ordinance to prevent this from happening, none was found. After much debate and discussion, however, the developer decided against using the barges.

Around the same time, it was announced that the Town of Huntington had lost its third attempt to lay claim to the title on the Centerport Mill Pond, which consisted of 20 acres between Mill Dam Road and Route 25A. The Appellate Division of the State Supreme Court decided that Titus Mill Pond, Inc., as descendants of the family that had claimed title since the 1860's, had ownership rights that superseded those of the Town. The battle between the family and the Town over title to the pond had started in 1898 when the Town made its first unsuccessful attempt to reclaim the pond. The pond, which was sold in 1985 to Donald Pius, remains a topic of bitter debate.

The Centerport community celebrated the newly constructed Our Lady Queen of Martyrs Catholic Church at the intersection of Prospect Road and Mill Dam Bridge, where the old Echo home was located. Shortly after the opening of the new church the original church was demolished to provide more parking for parishioners.

This Page Sponsored By:

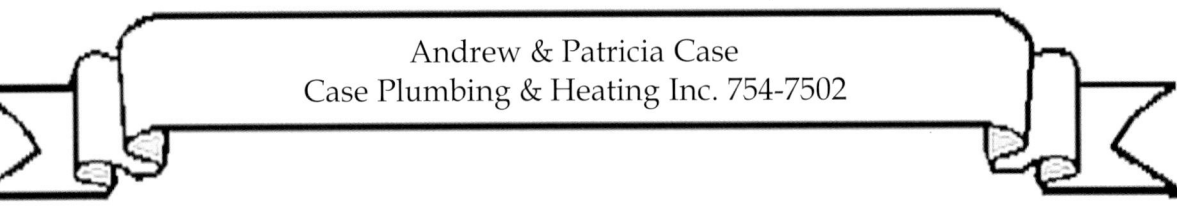

Andrew & Patricia Case
Case Plumbing & Heating Inc. 754-7502

Pete Gunther

Engine Co. #1
March, 1984
Rescue Squad: 1983-Present
Deputy Chief Fire Marshal:
1989-Present
Suffolk Co. Deputy Chief
Fire Coordinator: 1996-
Present
Chief: 1994-1995
1st Asst. Chief: 1992-1993
2nd Asst. Chief: 1990-1991
Hook & Ladder Co.:
Captain: 1988-1989
Lieutenant: 1987
E.M.T.
1990 Department Valor Award

Mary Gallagher Ryan
"Scarebear"

Eagle Truck Co. #1

March, 1984

Rescue Squad: 1984-
Present
Captain: Past
Lieutenant : Past
1st V.P.: 1997-1998
2nd V.P.: 1995-1996
E.M.T-D.

In June, the Department welcomed their first father-daughter team when Mary Gallagher, daughter of Ex-President and 25-year veteran Kevin, became the second female to enter the Department. Mary was a graduate of the very successful Cadet program, which enabled her to enter at age seventeen. Today, the Department has five father-daughter teams that proudly serve the Centerport community.

In November, Centerport was called to assist the Huntington Manor Fire Department with a fire that ripped through the Walt Whitman Mall on Route 110. Twelve fire departments assisted in controlling the fast moving blaze that destroyed seven stores and damaged 25 others. The fire began in a card shop near McCroy's and rapidly moved throughout the mall. Ten firefighters were taken to Huntington Hospital for smoke inhalation and one employee of Macy's was also treated. Luckily, the stores were not open at the time of the fire and the evacuation of the employees went smoothly.

In 1985, the Town of Huntington honored those volunteer firefighters from the township who had died in the line of duty with the dedication of a plaque. The plaque was donated by the Town of Huntington Fire Chief's Council and presented at Town Hall. Those firefighters honored on the plaque are Lou Lockwood, a member who died in 1930, Marion Harrison, Edward McGaul, Ernest Kanning, Joseph V. Machansky, Lloyd Coughlin, Thomas Kowalski, and John Cook. The plaque is permanently displayed in the entrance lobby of Town Hall and is inscribed, "Greater love hath no man than this that a man laid down his life for a friend."

Willing to sacrifice your life for another is what being a volunteer firefighter is all about. The badge

James Malico
"Rinny"

Engine Co. #1
September, 1984

Engine Co. #1
Captain: 1992-1993
Lieutenant: 1990-1991

Rescue Squad: 1984-1994
CPR

of a firefighter is the Maltese Cross, which is the symbol of protection and a badge of honor. The story of the Maltese Cross is hundreds of years old and began when a courageous band of Crusaders, known as the Knights of St. John, fought the Saracens for possession of the Holy Land. During these battles, they encountered a new weapon unknown at the time to European warriors. It was a simple, but horrible device and caused excruciating pain. The Saracens' weapon was, of course, fire. As the Crusaders advanced on the walls of the city, glass bombs containing naphtha struck them. When they became saturated with the highly flammable liquid, the Saracens hurled flaming torches into their midst. Hundreds of Knights were burned alive while others risked their lives to save their brothers in arms from dying a painful, fiery death. Those men became the first firemen and fellow Crusaders recognized their heroic efforts by presenting each hero with a badge of honor, similar to the cross firefighters wear today. Since the Knights of St. John lived on an island in the Mediterranean Sea named Malta, the cross came to be known as the Maltese Cross. The Maltese Cross means that the firefighter wearing it is willing to lay down his or her life for you, just as the Crusaders sacrificed their lives for their fellow man so many years ago. The Maltese Cross is a badge of honor for a firefighter, signifying that he or she works in courage, a ladder rung away from death.

The Department was called into action in September to assist neighbors when Hurricane Gloria rocked the area with severe winds, heavy rains, and high tides. Power went out at about 8:30 AM September 27, well before the storm actually arrived. Centerport residents scrambled to local stores to stock up on food and other needed supplies. As Hurricane Gloria approached, Chief

Top - Ice rescue Drill Bottom - The Scenic Mill Pond 1985

Cement truck overturn on Centerport Road

Feeley alerted the Department that a stand-by was necessary so that the apparatus could respond quickly in case of an emergency. Gloria hit the area head on. Hundreds of trees fell around Centerport, many into homes and parked cars. Boats along the shores were thrown on the beaches and into each other and many sank due to the high waves. Power lines were down all over the roads, which made access very dangerous. The firfighters made every attempt to clear the trees from the roads and wires in order to have a clear path in case of an emergency but Gloria was too big and powerful and thousands of people were left without power for days after she left. Schools were closed for most of the following week as clean-up crews from LILCO, Town of Huntington Highway, and the fire departments tried to uncover the area from the destruction of Hurricane Gloria.

1986 saw the New York Mets win their first Major League title since 1969, when they defeated the Boston Red Sox in seven games of the World Series and Steve Pribyl was Chief of the Department and James Reilly President. That same year, the New York Giants won their first Super Bowl Championship after beating the Denver Broncos.

Christopher Mahoney

Scuba Squad
March, 1985

Rescue Squad: 1985 - Present
Scuba Squad:
Captain: 1998
1st Lieutenant: 1997
2nd Lieutenant: 1995-1996
Rescue Squad:
Captain: 1994
Lieutenant: 1992-1993
Corresponding Secretary: 1995-1996
E.M.T.: 1986 - Present
A.E.M.T.: 1987 - Present
Paramedic: 1990 - Present
PADI Scuba; Adv. Open Water & Diver
Rescue Specialist Certifications- 1986,
87, 89
1992 Rescue Man of the Year Award

A new modular emergency medical ambulance, which replaced the Cadillac ambulance, was added to the fleet and joined the original modular unit which had been in service since 1977. Another significant apparatus addition was an aerial truck. The aerial (2-6-1) equipped with a KME body and 75-foot LTI ladder became the Department's first aerial truck. Used at fires and other emergencies, the truck has been an invaluable asset to the Department.

With the purchase of the new 2-6-1, the Board of Fire Commissioners needed to get rid of the old 2-6-1, a 1944 Mack Pumper. The Board of Fire Commissioners offered the truck to the Department for $1, which they eagerly accepted and today, "Old 2-6-1", has been fully restored and consistently wins prizes for best restored antique apparatus.

The response times by the police and Coast Guard were well below the acceptable level as the amount of water rescues increased in the area. In response to this need and under the leadership of Rescue Captain Jack Geffken, Centerport's first Dive Team was organized.

The physiological response in humans called the mammalian diving reflex, coupled with a quick response by the Dive Team increases the likelihood of survival. The mammalian diving reflex occurs when body temperature is significantly cooled due to being in the water, which results in bodily functions slowing down. This, in turn, increases the amount of time in which a successful rescue can occur. As soon as the Department arrives at the scene, the Dive Team enters the water in an organized, meticulous search for the victim. Once the victim is located and returned to the surface, members of the Rescue Squad perform CPR and other necessary medical procedures because, as the victim leaves the water, the mammalian diving reflex stops. Full advanced life support measures are taken to supply oxygen to the victim's brain thus increasing the chance of survival. Today, the Dive Team is equipped with it's own truck, inflatable boat, and two jet skis and can perform both water rescues and ice rescues.

Above - The new Ladder truck
Scuba training

In June, the relatively quiet Centerport community found itself the center of attention on the evening news and in local papers. On the evening of Wednesday, June 18 two people, were shot to death by an armed robber as they left the Tung Ting Restaurant on Centershore Road and Route 25A. The two individuals, a male and a female, were co-workers and had gone to Tung Ting to celebrate her decision to leave her job. As they walked to their car a man, armed with a handgun, demanded money from them. Before they could react, the robber shot both of them, killing her instantly. Police were on the scene immediately and notified the Department that medical attention

President James Reilly
1986-1987

Chief George Pribyl
1986-1987

was needed. Under the command of Chief Pribyl, the Department was able to keep the man alive long enough for him to give the police important information. Unfortunately, the desperate efforts of the Rescue Squad could not save him and he died two hours later in Huntington Hospital. No one was ever apprehended in the murder. Rumors, still around today, claim that the shooter was not a robber but was in fact a hired hit man. This version of the story, however, has never been confirmed.

The next day, another man was shot in the right forearm as he drove eastbound on Route 25A toward his home. After being shot, the man was able to drive his car to the Firehouse where he was treated and then transported to Huntington Hospital where he underwent surgery. This incident caused somewhat of a panic in Centerport, with rumors that both shootings were somehow related. Special units of the Suffolk County Police were called in and the police canvassed the area to locate the sniper. After only a few days, an arrest was made and the "sniper" turned out to be a teenage boy who was shooting at birds with his pellet gun in the area where the man was hit. The police confiscated the youth's rifle, which fired small, metal pellets and the boy was referred to family court.

The Department remained busy throughout the summer with the return of the tall ships to Long Island. A huge celebration was planned including a fireworks display and a parade of tall ships in Northport Bay. Due to the anticipated gridlock from the large amounts of spectators, the Town of Huntington declared a state of emergency for the area. As a precaution, the Centerport, along with Northport Fire Department, prepared a response plan in order to protect the surrounding areas. Fortunately, the plan never had to be utilized.

A string of fire and ambulance alarms in the fall kept the firefighters very busy. In November, an alarm was activated for a fire on Laurel Hill Road. The fire alarm in the house went off downstairs at about 7:45 PM as the homeowner was upstairs in the study which was next to the stairway and directly above the office that was on fire. She could not escape down the stairway due to the intense heat and smoke from the fire below so she exited another door, went through her study, her bedroom, and then down the staircase on the other side

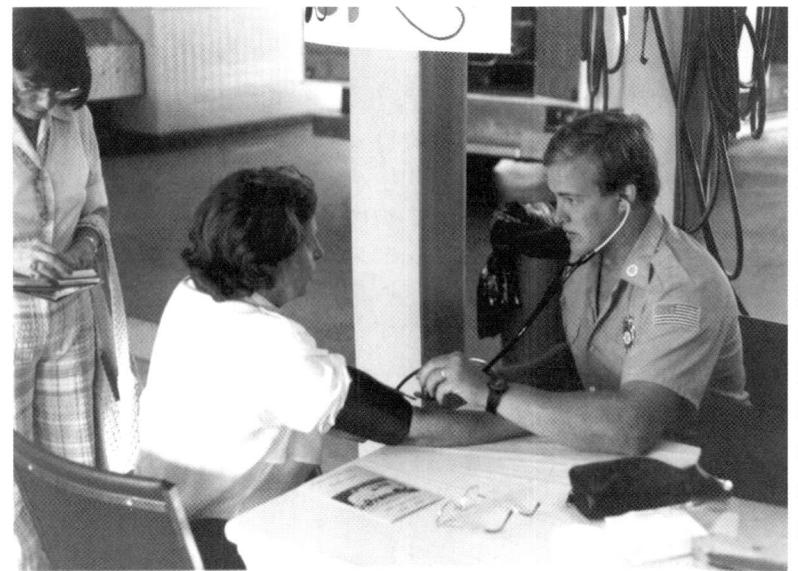

A resident getting her Blood Pressure checked at our open house

of the house, narrowly escaping. Flames and heavy smoke could be seen from blocks away and when Chief Pribyl arrived on the scene, the home, which was a large 16 room residence, was heavily charged with fire in about one-third of house. As the Department made an aggressive interior attack on the fire the floor above the burning office collapsed on to the lower level making the attack more difficult. The firefighters fought the blaze for more than an hour and a half before bringing it under control. The damage to the home was estimated at $50,000.00.

Raymond M. Kiesel
"Ray"

Eagle Truck Co. #1
March, 1987

Rescue Squad: 1987 -
Present

Scuba Squad:
Captain: 1990, 1997
Lieutenant: 1989

A.E.M.T.: -Present

1987 began with a dispute after the election for Fire Commissioner. In one of the most hard fought campaigns in the Centerport Fire District history, three term incumbent Gregory Sullivan edged challenger Ex-Chief Feeley by only 30 votes of the over 1,000 cast. The District's first order of business was the dismissal of active Feeley supporter Lieutenant Peter Gunther as Assistant Fire Inspector for the District, which created more controversy. At the first regular meeting of the new term, the Board was confronted by over 30 irate residents and members of the Department angry about the defeat of Ex-Chief Feeley and the ousting of Lieutenant Gunther. The most heated debate came when Chief Pribyl questioned why he had not been informed that an assistant fire inspector would not be appointed and the post eliminated.

Two weeks later, the Board held an open public forum to discuss the many allegations and problems brought up at the regular meeting. Over 100 residents, divided by their opinions, attended the meeting. A bitter debate erupted as firefighter Jerry Kubicki addressed the Board. The meeting finally ended late in the evening without closure from either side. As time went on, the frustration disappeared and the Department was able to move on.

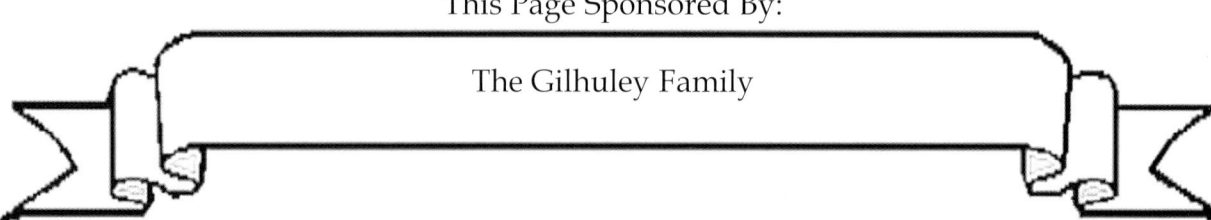

1987 - Halloween Party - An alarm occurred during the party - you can imagine the crew!
Below - Lightening caused this Little Neck Road Fire

In 1987 the Department and the Centerport community once again were faced with a society in transition. People were moving away from "blue - collar" jobs and seeking higher paying jobs in the business sector. Over half of all homes in the United States had cable television installed and this newer technology created the feeling of having to stay one step ahead of the competition. People worked longer hours at one or more jobs in an attempt to move up the corporate ladder. The Huntington Chief's Council held special meetings to discuss the problems of recruiting new members and also keeping the ones they had, as volunteers were moving to areas on eastern Long Island where housing was more affordable. Recruiting young people was not the problem. It was the middle-aged volunteer who didn't have the time to give to the fire departments that created the concern. The Chief's Council suggested adding "perks", but many feared that people would only join for the incentives. Other suggestions included having paid firefighters, but as Chief Pribyl indicated such a transition would double, if not triple the taxes of the residents. Unfortunately, these same concerns still exist today and it remains difficult to find a solution.

Even with the decline in the amount of active firefighters, the Department was still always able to provide the Centerport community with superior service and protection. In May, after a severe thunderstorm, an alarm was activated for a report of a house hit by lightening. Heavy smoke could be seen from across Centerport Harbor as the fire spread through the home. As the apparatus arrived at the Little Neck Road, house, the second floor and attic were fully involved with fire. Under the direction of Chief Pribyl, the Department made a "good stop" and prevented the fire from spreading to the rest of the house. The homeowner was so delighted that she wrote to The Long Islander about the Department's work, "The firemen arrived very quickly

Chief Paul Stevenson
1988-1989

President David McGovern
1988

and with expertise and consideration for my personal property, subdued the flames and smoke in about two hours. I am most grateful for their outstanding work."

Later that year, Centerport assisted the Northport Fire Department with an arson fire at a small business located on Main Street. Soon after, both departments joined in an effort to save the life of a 13-year old boy who was reported to have drowned in a lagoon at Sunken Meadow State Park. After several hours trying to locate the boy, 2nd Assistant Chief Andrew Mark and firefighter Tom Feeley found the 13-year-old. Visibility in the water was zero as both Chief Mark and Firefighter Feeley searched for the boy. Just as he was about to resurface, Chief Mark grabbed onto what he had thought was a submerged tree branch. As he examined the item, he realized that he was holding onto the leg of the boy. Chief Mark and Tom immediately brought the boy to the surface where other members of the Dive Teams brought him to shore. Unfortunately, the boy has been submerged too long. His family, however, was grateful that the Dive Teams were able to locate him.

Paul Stevenson was Chief and Dave McGovern became President in 1988 as the Department celebrated its 90th Anniversary. On August 31, the Dive Team was put into action once again. As residents of the Centerport and Northport communities were preparing for bed, a fire and explosion aboard the oil tanker, Fiona rocked the area. The Fiona was moored at the LILCO platform in Long

This Page Sponsored By:

Paul, Maureen, Christa, John, & Andrew Stevenson

Clifford R. Raynor

Engine Co. #2
January, 1988

Engine Co. #2:
Captain: 1998
Lieutenant: 1996-1997
President: 1995-1996
1st V.P.: 1993-1994
2nd V.P.: 1991-1992
Rescue Squad: 1989-Present
E.M.T-D: 1994 - Present
Scuba Squad: 1989 - Present
Captain: 1995
Lieutenant: 1993-1994

Island Sound about a mile off shore from the Northport plant. The sonic like boom of the explosion rattled windows and shook homes from Port Jefferson to Great Neck. The Northport Fire Department was first on the scene and immediately requested the assistance of the Centerport's Dive Team to locate seven men who were blown into the water from the explosion. The Coast Guard rescued six of the men, who suffered minor injuries, from the water. The seventh man, who had been closest to the explosion and was killed by the blast, was recovered four days later.

Rich Miltner

Engine Co. #1
March, 1988

Rescue Squad: 1990-Present
Engine Co. #1:
Captain: 1997-1998
Lieutenant: 1995-1996

Tom Feeley became President of the Department in 1989, a year in which several events occurred that were cause for celebration. First, the Department formed the 100th Anniversary Committee to begin the long preparation for the upcoming Centennial celebration in 1998. Then, 2-6-4 became the first vehicle dedicated to water rescue. The long anticipated arrival of the converted walk-in aluminum utility truck was finally a reality when it was delivered to the Department in 1989. In addition to 2-6-4, an Avon inflatable dive boat was also purchased to further support the Dive Team on all water and ice rescues.

Soon after, the Department received the newly refurbished 2-6-2 after a long reconstruction process. The Mack 1250 G.P.M. pumper, currently designated as 2-6-8, had received a complete makeover in order to comply with OSHA and the National Fire Protection Association (NFPA) requirements.

In September, the Department had one more reason to celebrate. On September 10, the drill team, commonly referred to as the "Hound Dogs", brought home 11 trophies from the Huntington Manor Fire Department Old-Fashioned Volunteer Firefighter Tournament. The trophies included 4th Place in buckets, 3rd Place in Efficiency, 2nd Place in Running Hose, Running Hook and Ladder, and Two into One. They were also awarded 1st Place in Running Hose Replacement, and, most important, the "Hound Dogs" took overall 1st Place for total points.

As a result of their superior efforts, the "Hound Dogs" received the Thomas J. Kowalski Memorial Trophy and the William "Buck" Spokre Memorial 10 year Leg Trophy for the most total points.

Also in the fall, one of the Department's members was once again honored for his selfless act of bravery during a fire. At 2:30 a.m. Captain Gunther, also a paid fire-fighter with FDNY, responded to a fire in Queens with Ladder Company 138. On this particular night, Pete had the job of being the O.V., or outside ventilator man. He saw a woman on the third floor holding her three-year old child and immediately screamed to her not to drop the child. Other firefighters were trying to reach the family by the stairway, but could not because of the intense fire that was out of control. Carrying a ladder to the third floor window, through flames and the smoke, and with the mother screaming, Pete was able to grab the child and bring him to safety. He then returned and brought the mother to the ground. He realized the father was still desperately trying to escape the fire so he returned to the blazing fire and found that the father was unable to escape because an air conditioner was in his way. Without thinking, and with amazing strength, Pete grabbed the air conditioner unit, dropped it to the ground, grabbed onto the father and carried him to safety.

Captain Pete Gunther, also a Staff Sergeant with the New York Air National Guard 106th Rescue Group, received the New York State Medal of Valor. Major General Charles S. Cooper III, Commander of the New York Air National Guard, presented him with this highest medal for bravery.

James C. Varese
"J.V."

Engine Co. #2
April, 1989

Rescue Squad: 1989-1995

Engine Co. #2:
Captain: 1996-1997
Lieutenant: 1994-1995
Cadet Advisor: 1989-1994

This Page Sponsored By:

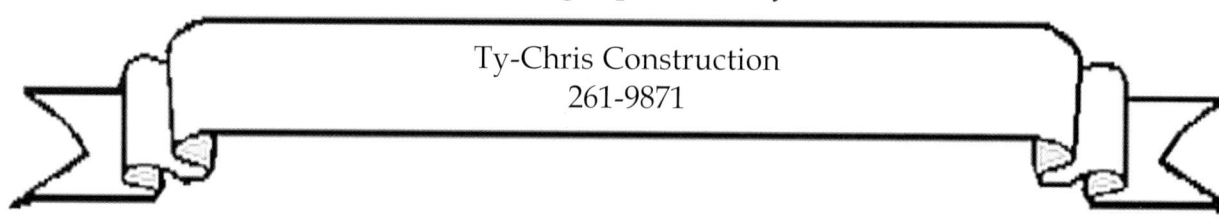

Ty-Chris Construction
261-9871

President Tom Feeley
1989-1990

Kevin D. Kustka
"KK"

Eagle Truck Co. #1
May, 1989

Rescue Squad: 1989-Present
Captain: 1998-Present

Engine Co. #2:
Captain: 1994-1995
Lieutenant: 1992-1993

Paramedic

1990 was a year in which the New York Giants won their second Super Bowl Championship in four years when they defeated the Buffalo Bills and Andrew Mark became Chief of the Department. The Department organized the "old 2-6-1" committee to research and complete the restoration of the 1944 Mack and the Ladie's Auxiliary celebrated their 50th Anniversary of dedicated service to the Department.

If anyone's tenure as Chief of the Department was tested, it was Chief Mark. 1990 was the beginning of a four-year period in which a sudden increase in the number of fires affected the Centerport community. Within his first year, Chief Mark was confronted with at least four severe blazes and countless "minor" incidences, as well as several mutual aids to neighboring departments.

In March, Centerport was called to assist neighboring Greenlawn Fire Department in an intense fire that ripped through the Samson Paper Bag Factory, it took many departments from Huntington Township several hours to control the blaze. Then in May, under the command of Chief Mark, the members made a "good stop" in fighting a stubborn fire on Bantry Court and, less than a month later, the Department fought two blazes within a day of each other on Little Neck Road and on Grant Street. Under the command of Chief Mark, firefighters conducted aggressive interior attacks on both fires, which were extinguished rapidly. Finally, in November Chief Mark commanded the Department during yet another fire on Laurel Hollow Road. It was truly a busy year.

Decorating the Firehouse

Chief Andrew Mark
1990-1991

President Patricia Bruce
1991-1992

Patricia Bruce became the first female to be elected President of the Department in 1991. 1991 brought with it the Gulf War and the nation was once again glued to the television as President George Bush and Congress declared war after Iraq's invasion of Kuwait. As the nation was trying to adjust to the crisis, so too was Centerport. In an effort to display support for the troops in the Gulf War, the Department decorated the Christmas tree in front of the Firehouse on Park Circle with yellow ribbons. On a more positive note, 1991 saw the end to 74 years of communist leadership in Russia and the possibility for democracy to flourish in the country.

Also in 1991, another of the Department's bravest was once again honored for his selfless act of bravery. Firefighter William Bokelmann was awarded the Valor Award for saving the life of a victim from a house fire. Firefighter Bokelmann was traveling in his car when he noticed smoke coming from a house. He immediately pulled over and attempted to gain access to the home.

Andrew Brian Mark

Engine Co. #1
May, 1991

Engine Co. # 1:
2nd Lieutenant: 1997-
1998

Cadet Advisor: 1998

Assisted by another individual, he entered the home where they were confronted by heavy, thick smoke. The other individual was overcome by smoke and had to retreat but Bill continued on, found the victim and pulled her to safety.

In March, the Department responded to an intense blaze on Bittner Lane. Upon arrival, the entire home was already fully involved with fire, and flames could be seen from hundreds of yards away as fire was venting from every window of the home. Fortunately, nobody was home and the blaze was extinguished within a few hours.

On May 16, Centerport was called to assist the Huntington Manor Fire Department in a tragic and deadly fire that destroyed McCrory's in the Walt Whitman Mall. This was the second fire in seven years to severely damage the Route 110 Mall. Huntington Manor Fire Department received the call at approximately 8:25 PM. Unlike the previous fire, the mall was occupied with shoppers and employees. It was reported that two people were unaccounted for and under the leadership of then 2nd Assistant Chief Peter Gunther, firefighters searched the interior of the

Chris Pribyl

Eagle Truck Co. #1
May, 1991

Robert A. Ciafardoni, Jr.
"Bobby"

Eagle Truck Co.#1
December, 1991

Eagle Truck Co. #1:
Captain: 1998-Present
1st Lieutenant: 1996-1997
2nd Lieutenant: 1995
Rescue Squad: 1991-
Present
E.M.T.: 1993-1995
1993 Fireman of the Year
Award

mall for the missing persons. 2nd Assistant Chief Gunther found the male victim in the middle of the isle fifteen to twenty feet from the entrance to the store and placed him over his shoulder and carried him out. 2nd Assistant Chief Gunther then went back into the store with a crew from the Syosset Fire Department to locate the other missing person. They found the succumbed woman's body underneath roofing debris about six feet from the stairwell. More than 250 firefighters from 13 departments, utilizing 47 pieces of apparatus fought the hot, smoky and intense fire for over five hours before it was declared under control.

Ice rescue training

Later that summer, firfighters responded to a blaze on Haven Court. Chief Mark was at the Firehouse that morning having a conversation with Houseman Craig Thomas when Craig noticed something that appeared to be smoke coming from the area of Haven Court. Minutes later, Chief Mark notified Thomas that they had a "working fire" on Haven Court. With mutual aid from Greenlawn, the Department fought the fire that severely damaged the home.

In less than a month, Centerport was once again called to assist another Department with a severe fire. Northport Fire Department was in need of assistance in the battle of an intense fire at the oyster factory located adjacent to the LILCO power station in Crab Meadow. Hundreds of firefighters from fire departments in Huntington and Smithtown fought the structure fire and brush fire for hours before it was finally brought under control. It was the second major "invitational" fire in less than two months to hit the Township of Huntington.

Less than a week later, the members responded to two fires in the same day. The first was an early morning fire on Arbutus Drive where Centerport assisted the Greenlawn Fire Department. The fire was so intense, that the paint on the first due pumper from Greenlawn was discolored from the radiant heat. Even with the hot weather and the hot smoky fire, both crews were able to make a great stop. Later that same day, at approximately 7:45 PM, the Department responded to a report of an unknown type of fire on Gina Drive. As Chief Mark arrived at the scene, he relayed to the Dispatcher to reactivate a signal 13 "working fire" as he observed fire rolling up the side of the house. After laying over 1500 feet of five-inch supply hose, the firefighters were able to extinguish the fire quickly and prevent it from extending into the interior of the home.

As most residents were just awakening, another fire hit the Centerport area in October. A report of a fire at the Centerport Marina located at the intersection of Mill Dam Road and Centershore Road was transmitted at 6:30 AM. As Chief Mark approached the scene he observed fire and heavy smoke billowing from the Marina. Ironically, firefighter Hal Bleiweiss lived directly across the street from the building and never noticed any smoke before he left home only 30 minutes earlier. Later this was explained when the fire was labeled suspicious and it was determined that accelerants were used in the blaze.

The Department was summoned to fight another fire on December 29, just two days before Chief Mark would retire from office. It was mid-morning and firefighters were at the Firehouse when smoke came billowing across Park Circle from the strip stores located on Little Neck Road. As firefighters ran across to investigate, they observed that the hair saloon located next to the Centerport Deli at the extreme south end of the stores was on fire and immediately notified Houseman Thomas to activate the alarm. As firefighters arrived, they were directed by Chief Mark to evacuate the adjacent stores, as patrons were unaware that the hair salon was on fire. Fortunately, nobody was injured in the fire and the Department was able to confine the fire to the hair salon with little damage to the deli.

Chief Gus Zeis
1992-1993

Gustave Zeis became Chief in 1992. Only nineteen days after taking office, Chief Zeis was put to work directing the Department's efforts at a fire. On January 19, at approximately 4:00 AM, a young boy awoke to thick, black smoke that filled his home on Westfield Drive. He crawled through the choking smoke and awakened his parents. All three family members crawled back to the son's bedroom where the father was overcome by the smoke. The mother broke the window and sent the boy next door to their neighbor who was a Halesite firefighter. The boy directed their neighbor to the window of the bedroom where his parents remained trapped. The neighbor forced open the window and entered the blazing home. By this time, the firefighters were notified of the blaze and sirens could be

Dog rescued by Firefighter Bill Sullivan

This Page Sponsored By:

John Giacoppi
"Chia Pet"

Engine Co. #1
January, 1992

Secretary: 1998
Rescue Squad: 1993 -
Present
Scuba Squad: 1993 -
Present
Engine Co. #1:
Lieutenant: 1997-1998
2nd Lieutenant: 1995-1996
1995 Firefighter of the
Year Award

Dan Knoph

Eagle Truck Co. #1
January, 1992

Rescue Squad: 1992 -
Present
Captain: 1/98-5/98
Lieutenant: 1996-1997

E.M.T.: Present
A.E.M.T.: Present

heard in the distance. The neighbor reached the unconscious victims and, one at a time rescued them from the burning home. As Chief Zeis arrived at the scene, all victims had safely escaped as heavy fire vented from the front of the home. The family and their rescuer were treated for abrasions and burns by the Rescue Squad and transported to Huntington Hospital. Chief Zeis commanded an aggressive attack on the raging blaze and was able to control the fire in a short time. At a ceremony at the Firehouse, both the boy and the Halesite firefighter were given medals and awards for their bravery and quick action in saving the lives of both parents.

Four more of Centerport's Ex-Chiefs were awarded with the prestigious "Chief Emeritus" status in 1992. Chief Zeis presented Ex-Chief Ken Klerk, Ex-Chief Ken Swan, Ex-Chief Earl Sammis and Ex-Chief William Wamp II with "Chief Emeritus" badges during respective Department meetings. Howard Wright was also honored with a "Service to the Community Award" for his 57 years of dedicated service to the Centerport community.

With concerns about health and fitness spreading throughout the nation, the Fire District decided it was time to take steps to protect its members. For the first time, the Department enacted mandatory physicals for all members in order to determine if members were physically capable of conducting firefighting activities without placing themselves in danger. Initially, many members were against the physicals, as they believed them to be an unnecessary invasion of their privacy. However, after realizing that the physicals were a means to protect them, few objected.

As the summer was coming to an end, the Department was hit with a tragic fire on

President James O'Donnell
1993-1994

The Annual Turkey Bowl - A football game between
Centerport & Greenlawn Fire Departments

Haven Court that claimed the life of an elderly woman. On August 7, as the members prepared to attend a funeral service for a Greenlawn firefighter, the fire erupted. As a nursing aid prepared breakfast in the kitchen, she noticed smoke coming from the bedroom of the home. The aid awakened the elderly male resident, but as she tried to assist his bedridden wife, the smoke and flames drove her back. Both the aid and elderly man were able to escape the fire and call for help. At the Firehouse, the scenario was very similar to the last fire on Haven Court when Chief Mark was Chief of the Department. Members were gathering in the rear of the Firehouse to depart for the funeral service, when one of them noticed smoke in the area of Haven Court. Just as they were going to inform the Dispatcher, the alarm phone rang. Chief Zeis arrived on the scene in seconds as flames erupted from the bedroom window. Neighbors immediately notified Chief Zeis that the elderly woman was still trapped inside. Although the firefighters were able to make a "great stop" on the fire, confining it to only two rooms within 30 minutes, the firefighters, unfortunately, were unable to save the woman.

Only four days later another fire erupted. A heavy storm had hit the area and the Department had responded to over two dozen calls as the storm took down trees, power lines, and flooded coastal areas. After the storm had passed, much of the Centerport area was left without power. As dusk neared, many residents began using candles and lanterns for light and the residents of Harned Drive were no different. A candle that was placed in a bedroom ignited a curtain and fire quickly spread throughout the bedroom and into

An old donated school bus was refurbished by the members of the Department

Christopher Heckel

Engine Co. #2
November, 1992

Rescue Squad: 1993 -
Present
Lieutenant: 1996- Present
E.M.T.
1994 Rescue Person of the
Year
Open Water Diver

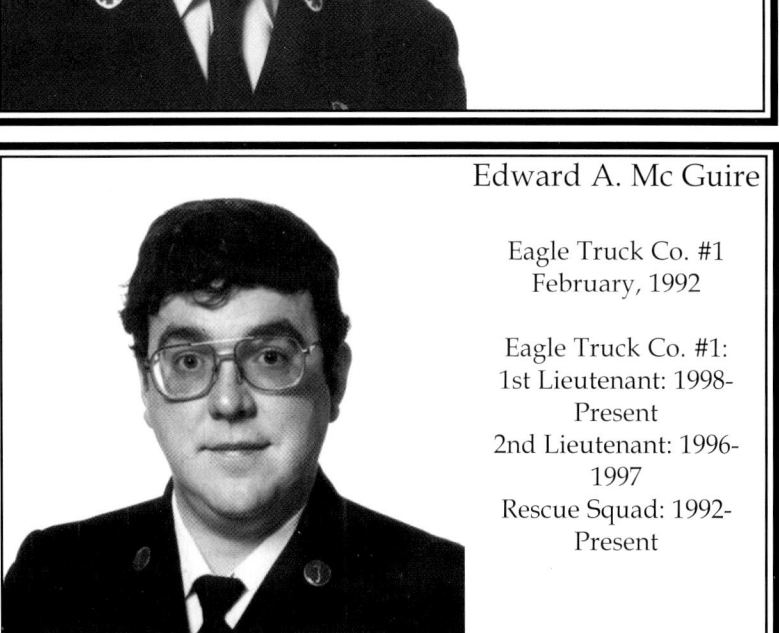

Edward A. Mc Guire

Eagle Truck Co. #1
February, 1992

Eagle Truck Co. #1:
1st Lieutenant: 1998-
Present
2nd Lieutenant: 1996-
1997
Rescue Squad: 1992-
Present

Joseph P. Mc Guire

Eagle Truck Co. #1
February, 1992

Rescue Squad: 1992 -
Present
Lieutenant: 1998
E.M.T.: 1994 - Present
1995 Rescue Man of the
Year Award

the next. At the same time the members were gathering for the monthly meeting. A resident from Harned Drive ran to the Firehouse, which was only blocks away, and notified Dispatcher Bruce Jennings of the fire. Coincidentally, firefighters from Station One located in Huntington Beach were in route to the Firehouse on Engine 2-6-2 for the meeting, when they noticed the smoke rising above the trees. Within minutes, the entire Department was on scene and fought the blaze. The fire was contained to the two bedrooms with little extension to the adjoining hallway.

James O'Donnell became President in 1993 as the Department celebrated 95 years of dedicated service to the Centerport community. With the fire epidemic still threatening the Centerport community, the Department braced itself for another long year. In March the first fire erupted on a cold and snowy evening. As Chief Zeis and 1st Assistant Chief Gunther arrived on Merriwood Court, flames were raging 45 feet above the home. The homeowners were away on vacation and the fire had been burning for hours before it finally broke through a second story window and was noticed. As firefighters arrived, the glow from the intense blaze could be seen from hundreds of yards away. Firefighters fought the stubborn fire for hours before it was finally extinguished.

In May, the firefighters were put back into action again. The Department had just returned from a false alarm when a report of a fire on Laurel Hill Road was received. As Chief Zeis arrived, smoke was billowing from the basement of the home and he immediately declared a "working fire". Due to the distance between the road and the home, it was necessary to lay long lengths of hose in order to fight the blaze. The Department was able to make a "good stop" and confined the fire to the basement area. Ironically, the homeowner

Cary Smolcnop
"Smokey"

Engine Co. #1
February, 1993.

Rescue Squad: 1994-
Present

was the son of the woman who escaped a fire at the same location in 1986 when Steve Pribyl was Chief.

Only a month later, a report of a fire at the Country Lake Nursing Home on Centershore Road put a scare into the Department. At approximately 1:00 in the afternoon the alarm phone rang in the Firehouse and the report of a structure fire at the Country Lake Nursing Home was sounded over the in-house paging system as the Dispatcher activated the sirens. Normally, fire alarms for the nursing home are received via a central alarm system, therefore, firefighters knew this was the "real thing". As Chief Zeis arrived on the scene, smoke billowed across the rear parking lot, the Greenlawn Fire Department was immediately summoned for mutual aid. As the first firefighters arrived, Chief Zeis ordered the search and evacuation of all the workers and residents while the next crew that arrived was ordered to advance a hoseline to the basement to attack the fire. Both procedures went very smoothly and all employees and residents were quickly evacuated and the fire extinguished.

Bryan Murphy

Eagle Truck Co. #1
March, 1993

Deputy Chief Chaplin
1993 - Present

Cadet Advisor 1993-1995

Scuba Squad:
Captain 1996-1997
Lieutenant 1995

Christopher Cunningham

Engine Co. #1
May, 1993

Later that summer, Centerport received two new pumpers to add to its fleet of apparatus. The twin "alert series" pumpers, that were designated as 2-6-2 and 2-6-3 and placed in Station One and Headquarters respectively, had enclosed six man cabs as required by N.F.P.A. standards. The pumpers were specially ordered with a shorter wheelbase and truck length to enable the pumpers to fit within the current Firehouse and aid maneuvering in some of Centerport's narrow streets. In addition to the two new pumpers, under the advise of Deputy Chief Doctor Geffken and the Rescue Officers, the Department also placed a First Responder vehicle into service for

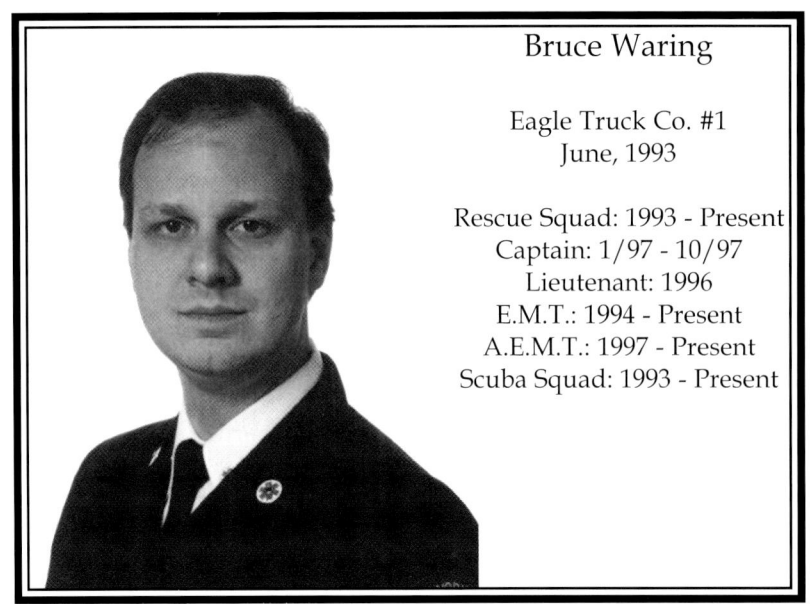

Bruce Waring

Eagle Truck Co. #1
June, 1993

Rescue Squad: 1993 - Present
Captain: 1/97 - 10/97
Lieutenant: 1996
E.M.T.: 1994 - Present
A.E.M.T.: 1997 - Present
Scuba Squad: 1993 - Present

quicker responses to medical emergencies. When a Chief was not using one of the three cars, it would be loaded with necessary medical emergency equipment and used by an Emergency Medical Technician (E.M.T.) in order to respond directly to a scene and conduct patient care before the ambulance arrived. Currently, Centerport has a separate First Responder vehicle that is dedicated to this purpose. With the use of this vehicle, the Department has been able have trained personnel respond quicker to medical emergencies.

Centerport ended the year with two more fires. The first occurred on Adams Street at approximately 12:00 noon. As 2nd Assistant Chief Heglund arrived at the scene, he announced that he had smoke showing at the residence. The fire was located in the basement and was quickly spreading. Fortunately for the homeowner, the intense heat of the blaze melted a plastic fitting on a water pipe, which broke open and confined the fire. Firefighters quickly advanced a line into the basement and extinguished the remaining fire within minutes.

**Chief Peter Gunther
1994-1995**

The second fire occurred on Paul Revere Lane. This time, 2nd Assistant Chief Heglund was alerted for a call for smoke in the area of Route 25A and Stony Hollow Road. As he was unable to locate the cause of the smoke in that area, Chief Heglund decided to search the area of Paul Revere. As he approached Paul Revere Lane he noticed smoke and notified the dispatcher that there was a house fire. The blaze apparently began in the kitchen and extended to the second floor through an air conditioning vent, where the firefighters stopped it with an aggressive interior attack. The fire, which was confined to an upstairs closet, gutted the kitchen and caused severe heat and smoke damage throughout the home. It was brought under control in about 50 minutes, assisted by Greenlawn and Northport Fire Departments.

Peter Gunther became Chief in 1994 the year in which the New York Rangers won their first Stanley Cup Championship since 1940. It wasn't long under Chief Gunther's command before the Department was put to work fighting another blaze. On January 16, the members were alerted to a fire on Laurel Hill Road, which was the third fire in under a year to occur within this area. Firefighters made an aggressive interior attack and the blaze was brought under control in

Andrew F. Beyer
"Gump"

Engine Co. #1
March, 1994

Rescue Squad: 1994-
Present

approximately 50 minutes.

As the winter progressed, the local area was hit with many snowstorms that left the Centerport community under a blanket of snow and ice. On February 1, the dispatcher received a call at about 10:00 AM from a woman who had been walking along Centerport Beach. She reported that she had seen a man with a clam rake walking on the ice in the frozen harbor about 20 feet from shore, however, when she looked back again a few minutes later, the man had disappeared. Another man who was across the harbor at Fleets Cove Beach confirmed the woman's report, saying that he too had seen a man on the ice but didn't see him leave. Centerport F.D. and the Huntington Harbor Patrol were first on the scene. Due to the drifting snow and an ice-choked harbor, Chief Gunther requested mutual aid from the Greenlawn, Northport, Halesite, Huntington, and Cold Spring Harbor Fire Departments and they were later joined by divers from the marine recovery unit of the Suffolk County Police.

Using a buoy as a marker, divers searched for the man in freezing waters, fanning out in ten foot circles. Rescue personnel also searched along the shore as police canvassed the homes, which faced the beach across the harbor. Almost two hours later, a man in one of the houses said he had seen a man matching the description of the clammer safely leave the ice. Although the clammer was not found, the search was called off after it was determined that the "missing man" may have simply left the ice without being noticed. Later that week, it was confirmed that the clammer had left the ice safely, and any concerns the Department had were put to rest.

As the bitterly cold winter continued, the members celebrated some significant achievements. Peter Reilly, who was, and still is, an active member, received the status of "Honorary Chief" by Chief Gunther for his 40 years of service. In addition, Harry Burr became the seventh member to be awarded the status of "Chief Emeritus" by the Department.

John Stevenson

Engine Co. #2
September, 1994

Rescue Squad: 1996-
Present

E.M.T.

Spring arrived, and as the residents were thawing out from the harsh winter, the Centerport community was hit with a fire the likes of which had not been seen in 10 years. April 18 was a quiet day before the Department was alerted to a fire at Rockhoppers Restaurant on Centershore Road. When Dispatcher Thomas gazed over the Mill Pond from the rear of the Firehouse, he could see heavy smoke billowing from the area of the restaurant. As Chief Gunther arrived on the scene, he encountered a heavy fire, which was quickly spreading throughout the restaurant. He immediately requested mutual aid from the Greenlawn and Northport Fire Departments.

The fire, which had started in the kitchen, spread into the ductwork and rapidly spread into the common cockloft of two adjoining buildings. As the blaze worsened, Chief Gunther requested additional assistance from Halesite,

Rockhoppers Fire

Now slated to become a park

Huntington, and East Northport. The two adjoining buildings, which contained offices, were heavily damaged by fire. A third building was saved due to an aggressive interior attack by the 150 firefighters who remained on the scene fighting the spectacular blaze until it was brought under control at approximately 5:30 PM. Rockhoppers and the adjoining collection agency was significantly destroyed by the fire, which caused approximately $100,000.00 in damage.

Due to increasing concern about potential major fires, Chief Gunther headed a town-wide drill at the Vanderbilt Museum. Over 200 firefighters from all over the Town of Huntington responded with about 43 pieces of apparatus, including engines, ladder trucks, heavy rescue trucks, tankers and ambulances. The drill's focus was to familiarize the firefighters with the museum layout in the event of a major fire or incident. Due to the newer and larger fire apparatus, accessibility to the various parts of the mansion's narrow areas was tested, as was the available water supply. The drill proved to be a valuable training and learning experience for all the fire departments involved.

Open house at C.F.D.

As the fire epidemic cooled down, the Department's softball team began to heat things up. After a very successful regular season, Centerport met the Greenlawn Fire Department in a best of three games final for the Huntington Township Fireman's Softball League (HTFSL) Championship. After Centerport won the first game, Greenlawn came back to win the second. It was now down to a third and final game to determine who would be champion. Both teams battled for dominance in less than perfect weather of fog and misty rain. In the later innings, Centerport started hitting the ball with power and Greenlawn unraveled. The Department went on to win and became the 1994 H.T.F.S.L. Champions. The Championship team included team manager Tom Boyd, Chris Cunningham, Jim Malico, John Giacoppi, Rich Miltner, Kevin Dearie, Jim Varese, Andy Beyer, Bob Ciafardoni, Mike Zeis, Tom Liebler, Ed McGuire, Andy Case, Scott Sammis, and Kevin Kustka.

H.T.F.S.L. Champs

Cliff Raynor became President in 1995 the year the Department was featured on a popular morning television wake-up show. The focus of the show was the fire museum located in the Firehouse on Park Circle. The unique and colorful museum is filled with historic items and memorabilia from the Department's past and is open to the public. The original hand pumper is the centerpiece of the museum and along with the large quantity of firefighting equipment, scrapbooks, trophies and

other items contained in the museum, visitors can easily visualize Centerport's rich history and historic firefighting past. A lot of the material in the museum relates in some way to the Department's history with the Vanderbilt family. For example, hanging on the wall of the museum is a picture of the first ambulance, which reads, "Vanderbilt Rescue Squad." That name, however, was never officially used, although Vanderbilt was willing to donate one million dollars to the Firehouse if it had been. The offer was ultimately rejected.

The team that transported the mummy

Later that year, on Halloween, the Department transported a 3,000-year-old Egyptian mummy by ambulance to Huntington Hospital for the Vanderbilt Museum as part of a project, by a Long Island University Egyptologist, to preserve and study the mummy. The mummy, which was acquired by William K. Vanderbilt II in 1931, spent 63 years in the Vanderbilt Museum. At the hospital the mummy underwent a series of x-rays and a CAT scan in the hopes of finding answers to the many

mysteries that still surrounded Egyptian mummies. The mummy was and is, without a doubt, the oldest "patient" the Rescue Squad ever transported to Huntington Hospital.

Ex-Captain Bill Casey, a member for over 30 years, was presented with the Lifesaving Award in recognition for saving the life of an attempted suicide victim. While working at Bethpage State Park, Bill was alerted by a patron that a car was parked outside the picnic area with a semi-conscious female inside. Bill found the car locked and running with a hose connected from the exhaust pipe into the car. He talked the 18 year-old into releasing the car's lock and got fresh air to the young lady. The Bethpage Fire Department transported the young woman to a nearby hospital where she fully recovered. At the ceremony, Bill was also presented with a certificate of recognition from the Long Island State Park Region.

President Cliff Raynor
1995-1996

During 1995, the residents of Centerport and Northport, as well as motorists who traveled through the area, were subjected to a deadly road condition on a long length of

The Rescue team

Route 25A. The New York State of Department of Transportation (DOT) had allowed contractors to use an asphalt mixture in which all the rocks were dolomite, a rock long known for its tendency to "polish" or become slippery under heavy wear and tear. After the DOT paved Route 25A with this mixture, the rate of car accidents quadrupled. Due to this significant increase in the amount of car accidents between Woodbine Avenue and Centershore Road, the DOT was severely criticized. At one accident, Chief Gunther closed down Route 25A for three hours, refusing to open it until the DOT sanded the road and pronounced it safe.

Under the pressures of Chief Gunther, Northport Police Chief Robert Howard, local politicians, and the local media, the DOT began emergency testing of the roadway. The DOT determined Route 25A to be unsafe and immediately took steps to pave the road with suitable asphalt.

Later that year, members of the Department teamed together to save the life of a brother firefighter. On July 28, firefighters Jim Pribyl and Brian Caiola were enjoying a warm summer day boating with friends in Northport Bay. As Jim was tubing behind the boat, he was suddenly hit by a wave, which tossed him into the water in such a violent way that he injured both his head and abdomen. Brian, who later went on to receive the Department's Valor Award and Suffolk County Class III Medal of Valor for his heroic efforts, noticed that Jim was in trouble and immediately jumped into the water to keep Jim afloat. Brian ordered the others on the boat to go for help as he held on to Jim and as they both drifted dangerously toward the Long Island Sound. Soon after, the Firehouse was notified that one of their own was injured and Chief Gunther instructed divers and medical personnel to execute the rescue. Captain Kevin Dearie, Deputy Chief Doctor Jack Geffken, Ex-Chief James Feeley, and Lieutenant John Giacoppi took immediate steps to rescue Jim. As they approached the area, both Brian and Jim were quickly being swept away by the strong current. Jeopardizing his own safety, Brian remained in the water with Jim. After they were rescued and immediate care was given, both Jim and Brian were brought to shore after which Jim was

transported to the University Medical Center at Stony Brook by helicopter. Jim was released the next day having suffered from hypothermia, bruised intestines and a slight concussion. It is a brotherhood like this that makes being part of the volunteer fire service all worth while.

In August, Centerport would once again be called to join the brotherhood of firefighters in a gargantuan firefighting effort. It started on August 24 and turned out to be the worst fire in New York State in the last 50 years. Over 6000 acres of Pine Barrens were destroyed by a raging brush fire that swept through the

The Wild Fires as seen from the windshield of our pumper
Photo courtesy of John Giacoppi

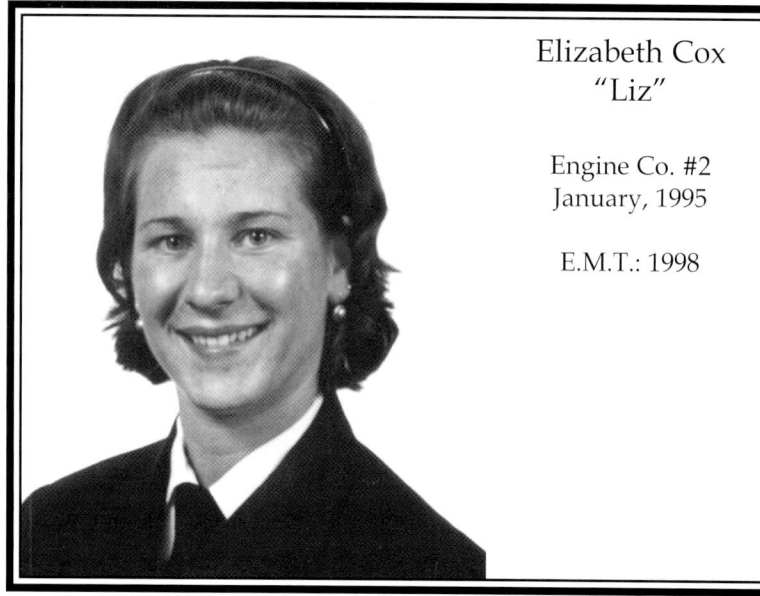

Elizabeth Cox
"Liz"

Engine Co. #2
January, 1995

E.M.T.: 1998

Hamptons in Eastern Long Island. The famous "Sunrise Fires" began at 11:30 AM on a day that would seem to last almost a week. Fueled by drought like conditions, the fire grew to heights of eighty feet and one and a half miles long. The blaze jumped the four-lane Sunrise Highway twice as it created its own energy and became a rolling fireball. Smoke could be seen for miles and in places, day turned to "night" while residents, in some areas, had to be evacuated.

All 110 Suffolk County fire departments were called to fight the blaze along with all 97 Nassau County fire departments, as well as paid firefighters from F.D.N.Y., Westchester and New Jersey. It was the first time since 1904 that the New York City Fire Department had come to Long Island to fight a blaze. In addition to the hundreds of metropolitan area firefighters, air guard units from across the nation were also called. Along with the 6,000 acres consumed by the fire, the fire damaged two residential homes, several commercial businesses and the Westhampton train station. The estimated two thousand plus firefighters battled the blaze for three days before it was declared under control on

Brian Caiola

Engine Co. #1
February, 1995

Rescue Squad: 1995 - Present

1995 Department Valor Award

James Michael Pribyl

Engine Co. #1
May, 1995

August 26. In addition to being fought from the ground, several helicopters and fixed wing small aircraft were used to dump water on the blaze from above. Large aircraft capable of carrying 3,000 gallons of water a flight arrived two days late and, although they were used, had little effect on the firefight. President Clinton, at the request of Governor Pataki declared the area a federal disaster. Although the fire consumed a 12 mile square area, the limited damage and lack of serious injury was considered nothing short of miraculous for a fire of that magnitude.

Caroline Feeley

Eagle Truck Co. #1
November, 1995

Rescue Squad: 1995 -
Present
Scuba Squad - Present
Firefighters' Assn. State
of New York (FASNY) -
Present

Todd M. Lewis, Sr.

Engine Co. # 2
December, 1995

The words of Congressman Michael Forbes made on the floor of the House of Representatives speak for themselves. He said, "The determination shown in beating back an ever-shifting wall of fire, driven by unpredictable and finicky winds, is testament to the excellent training and dedication for which our professional volunteer firefighters have become known. You (firefighters) dug deep within yourselves to find the strength to carry on in the face of over-whelming odds, putting the health and welfare of each of us in the community ahead of your personal safety, to do a job and do it spectacularly. Your unselfish service to our community exemplifies the true spirit of volunteerism."

"We are pleased for the country, state and federal support that came to Eastern Long Island during the blaze but, quite honestly, the fire was extinguished because of the on-ground, tactical fire-fighting rendered by each and every man and woman of our local fire departments. It was this world class effort, by the best and the bravest, that brought an end to this disaster with a minimum of injuries and no loss of life. You made that possible. You are all solid-gold true blue American heroes. All of Long Island thanks you!"

The Department ended 1995 with a fire, an event that had not occurred in Centerport for over a year and a half. It was Thanksgiving Day and the members were enjoying Thanksgiving dinner when a fire on Daphne Lane was reported. When 2nd Assistant Chief Robert Simpson arrived on the scene he announced that he had heavy smoke showing as the occupants of the home safely evacuated. Seconds later the windows and skylight of the bedroom gave way and fire erupted from the interior of the home. As firefighters arrived at the scene, they were confronted with a heavy fire that consumed the bedroom, the adjoining hallway and the stairs leading up to the second floor. Because of the flammable substance used on the treated wood floors of the home, firefighters encountered a wall of fire at the bottom of the stairs. With an aggressive interior attack, the fire-fighters were able to battle up the stairs, into the hallway and to the origin of the fire. Within about 40 minutes, the fire was under control. The bedroom and hallway sustained heavy fire damage but the rest of the second floor only suffered from smoke and heat damage due to the "great stop" by the firefighters.

Chief Paul Heglund
1996-1997

Paul Heglund became Chief in 1996 and was initially confronted with a rash of motor vehicle accidents, many which required the use of the "Jaws of Life" or Hurst tool, as it is more commonly referred to in the fire service.

It was not until February that Chief Heglund was "tested" as Chief for a fire. It was cold on Sunday, February 4 when the members and Chief Heglund were notified of the first fire of the year in a boiler room on Laurel Hill Road. As 1st Assistant Chief Simpson and the ladder truck, 2-6-1, arrived, light smoke was visible from the home. Firefighters immediately investigated the boiler room where they observed fire against the wall between the boiler and the exterior wall. 1st Assistant Chief Simpson ordered a line to the boiler room to extinguish the fire, but, as the attack line was in place to hit the flames, fire erupted from the wall of the second floor immediately above the boiler room. A second line was stretched to the second floor to attack the rapidly spreading fire. As a result of their ability to command and the organized tactics of the firefighters, the fire was confined to the boiler room and the exterior wall of the home.

In the Spring, the Department found itself in the middle of a debate over the Fire District's proposal for a $1.55 million expansion to the Firehouse. As the Fire District was trying to resolve the alarming deficiencies in the overcrowded Firehouse that were in violation of OSHA recommendations, concerned residents of the Centerport community were trying to keep taxes from increasing. The District proposed the purchase of the building adjacent to the Firehouse. Part of the building would be converted into a double-bay extension to the Firehouse and the other part would be used for firematic and public purposes. The total cost was estimated to be about $67.00 per year for the average homeowner for a total of ten years.

The Fire District held an open debate to discuss the plans of the Fire District and to air the concerns of the Centerport community. Over 150 residents crowded into the meeting at the Firehouse in order to participate in the open forum. The large turnout was attributed to the amount of coverage given to the issue in the local papers, informational pieces mailed by the Fire District and the lobbying by the "Concerned Citizens of Centerport". On May 2, over 1,000 Centerport residents came out to vote, which was the heaviest turnout for any vote in recent memory. The

Firefighters Feeley & Reilly

Andrew Stevenson

Engine Co. #2
January, 1996

Rescue Squad: 1996-1998

E.M.T.

referendum was defeated. The outcome was neither seen as a victory for the Centerport community or a defeat for the Department. The question will come up again, as new equipment will continue to take up the already limited space, and an answer will need to be found.

On May 10, just 8 days after the vote, the Department responded to three separate motor vehicle accidents including one that involved a fatality. The Department responded to the first accident at about 3:00 AM when a car struck a tree and then a pole at the intersection of Centershore Road and Centerport Road.

The driver of the car was pinned in the wreckage and was freed in about 20 minutes using the "Jaws of Life" and cutters to remove both doors and the roof of the vehicle. The Rescue Squad immediately attempted to revive the driver by using Advanced Life Support, or ALS, defibrillating the driver twice. Unfortunately, even the extraordinary efforts did not save the driver who later died in Huntington Hospital.

The Department responded to the second collision, which involved two cars at 1:45 PM at the intersection of Route 25A and Centershore Road. 1st Assistant Chief

Erin Reilly

Engine Co. #2
February, 1996

Nicholas Feeley
"Nick"

Eagle Truck Co. #1
June, 1996

Simpson requested assistance from the Greenlawn Fire Department and the members once again utilized the Hurst tool, or "Jaws of Life", to open the door on one of the cars in order to free the victim trapped inside. Two female drivers were transported to Huntington Hospital with neck and back injuries. The day of accidents ended shortly after 10:00 PM with a head on collision at Little Neck Road and Route 25A. Four victims sustained minor injuries.

Centerport has always prided itself on its high level of training and its consistent efforts to be prepared for a variety of potential disasters. In keeping with this

Motor Vehicle Accident
Right - Patient going via helicopter to a trauma center
(The patient recovered)

philosophy, the members conducted a drill that simulated a kitchen fire that spread to the 2nd and 3rd floors of the Greentree Manor Adult Home on Cherry Lane. Multiple injuries consisting of smoke inhalation, burns, fractures and trauma were also simulated. The drill, under the command of Chief Heglund, brought a response of 100 fire and rescue personnel from Centerport as well as the Greenlawn, Halesite, Northport, East Northport, Cold Spring Harbor, and Commack Fire Departments. The drill utilized 15 pieces of emergency apparatus including engines, aerial ladder trucks, heavy rescue trucks,

and ambulances. Responding firefighters entered the home and rescued "victims" who were actually Centerport and East Northport Fire Cadets with realistic looking injuries. Rescue squad members transported the "victims" to Huntington Hospital where a training drill was held for the hospital's Emergency Room certification. Chief Heglund was quoted as saying the drill was, "successful due to the dedication and response of our volunteer firefighters and support from our neighboring departments."

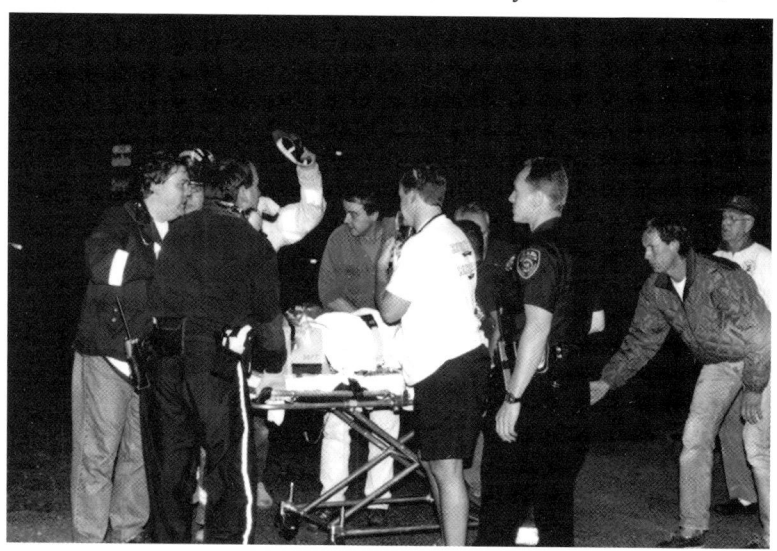

Michael Mc Carrick

Engine Co. #2
December, 1996

Rescue Squad: 1996-
Present

In June, Centerport recognized a long time friend and associate of the Department with an honorary tribute. Steve Silverman, a veteran photographer for Centerport, as well as other Town of Huntington Fire Departments and Fire News, was appointed as a Deputy Chief for Photography. Steve was recognized for his many years of dedication to the Department in particular and the fire service in general.

Later that summer, the Department celebrated the arrival of a new ALS ambulance and two jet skis that were donated by Kawasaki.

David Knoph
"Private Pile"

Eagle Truck Co. #1
December, 1996

Rescue Squad: 1997 -
Present

A great loss was suffered in 1996 when Ex-Chief Louis Scarduzio, a respected friend and colleague to many, suddenly died from heart failure. The Rescue Squad was summoned to assist Ex-Chief Scarduzio but, unfortunately, even their greatest efforts to revive him failed. Ex-Chief Scarduzio's sudden passing elicited a tremendous outpouring of sympathy for his family. A full firematic burial was held at Northport Rural Cemetery on Sandy Hollow Road.

William Penny became President of the Department in 1997 and after a quiet

ending to 1996 with respect to fires, began the year with an early morning blaze on Salem Ridge Drive. It was a cold, Saturday morning on February 8 when the dispatcher received the alarm for the fire at 2:16 AM. A natural gas-fed barbecue in the backyard, which inadvertently had been left on, started the fire. As the residents slept, the fire spread to the eaves of the house and into the attic. Luckily, the residents were awakened by the fire alarm system installed in their home. When Chief Heglund arrived at the scene, flames were erupting into the sky from the rear portion of the home's

Katherine Hahn
"Katy"

Engine Co. #2
January, 1997

roof and he immediately transmitted a "working fire" as the fire rapidly spread throughout the attic. Firefighters fought the fire with four hoselines stretched to various sections of the home and had the fire under control within 50 minutes. This scenario stresses the value of having a fire alarm system that works in the home, which, due to the severity of this fire, definitely prevented injuries and or death.

As the year progressed, the Department eagerly anticipated the arrival of its 100th Anniversary in 1998. Countless meetings were held, as the members made the necessary arrangements for the many festivities scheduled to take place during the celebration. In addition, the

Andrew Heglund
"Andy"

Engine Co. #2
January, 1997

George Ello

Engine Co. #2
May, 1997

Department was doing some early celebrating as the restoration of "old 2-6-1" was finally completed. The availability of a first responder vehicle (2-6-80), 24 hours a day added to the excitement, as the Rescue Squad received the vehicle for its Emergency Medical Technicians.

The Department also received a new Power Hawk "Hurst" Tool to aid in the extrication of victims involved in vehicle accidents. The Power Hawk, the first of its kind to be used in this area, is a smaller

Memorial Day - Work then Play

version of the "Jaws of Life". Engineers that developed the wing mechanism on the F-14 fighter jet used by the U.S. Navy designed the Power Hawk. Rather than being powered by hydraulic fluid like its larger counterpart, the lightweight, compact Power Hawk utilizes a battery to energize the powerful arms. The Power Hawk proved itself a very useful and necessary tool during motor vehicle accidents and other emergencies.

In April, Ex-Chief Edwin Seim received the prestigious status of Chief Emeritus in recognition of his tenure as Chief and his 40 years of active service. In addition, Connie Zink was presented with the

Above - House fire on Salem Ridge - started by a BBQ
Right - Truck Co. annual car show at the beach

Mike Bruno

Eagle Truck Co. #1
February, 1998

award and status of "Honorary Chief" for achieving 40 years of active service.

Just six months later, Ex-Chief Edwin Seim died after a short battle with leukemia. The Department was shocked by his passing and immediately took . steps to support his grieving family. Chief Heglund made preparations for a full firematic funeral for the widely admired Ex-Chief. A huge turnout of fire-fighters from all over Huntington Township and other communities gathered at the firematic wake at Nolan's Funeral Home in Northport to pay tribute to Ex-Chief Seim. During the funeral,

members in full Class "A" uniforms flanked Ex-Chief Seim and stood by throughout the services. Ex-Chief Seim was then transported aboard "old 2-6-1" to the Firehouse. There, the funeral procession paused for the traditional sounding of the fire siren as members of the Northport Fire Department, dressed in full firefighting turn-out gear, gave a final salute. The procession resumed and a full firematic burial was held at the Long Island National Cemetery in Pinelawn. At the November regular monthly meeting, the members observed a moment of silence as Ex-Chief Earl Sammis sounded the fire gong in the front of the Firehouse in honor of Ex-Chief Seim.

Kevin Feeley

Eagle Truck Co. #1
May, 1998

Brian Feeley

Eagle Truck Co. #1
May, 1998

Centerport had assisted Greenlawn in October, fighting a spectacular fire at the Oak Tree Dairy on Elwood Road, which required the assistance of ten neighboring fire departments. Flames, however, had happily not been seen in Centerport since February. It was Christmas day, and while many firefighters were enjoying their holiday with family members, a report of a fire on Hayes Place was dispatched. As Chief Heglund arrived close to the scene, smoke billowed across the Huntington Beach area creating a fog like atmosphere. Once on the scene, flames could be seen erupting out of the windows of the unoccupied home and he

Dan Dillon

Engine Co.#1
July, 1998

Above - Oak Tree Dairy   Below - Hayes Place

immediately declared a "working fire". The first fire-fighters entered the home and attacked the blazing fire. A rapid intervention team was requested from the Greenlawn Fire Department to assist as firefighters made progress confining the fire. Even though the fire occurred on Christmas day, many firefighters responded to the blaze. Chief Heglund was proud of the members he was able to command for one last time during his term as Chief. In 1998 Robert Simpson became Chief and the 100th Anniversary committee was gearing up for a busy year. In the rest of the United States El Nino caused a mild winter with widespread flooding problems. LILCO was taken over by LIPA, John Glenn returned to space at age 77, Mark McGuire broke Roger Maris' 37 year old record (61) by hitting 70 home runs in one season, and the Yankees won the World Series. The May Department meeting may have started out like all the others but it didn't end up that way. At 9pm a lightning storm moved through the area causing Centerport to receive and respond to 5 calls for houses hit by lightening. A house on Renwick Drive sustained a lightening hit that entered the houses electrical system and exited in the laundry room causing a fire. When the Engine Co. connected to the fire hydrant they where suprised to find that nothing came out!! The lightening bolt also traveled out into the water main causing it to blow about 50 feet from the house making the hydrant inoperable.

The new Heavy Rescue Truck

The homeowners quick actions combined with the quick response kept the damage to a minimum. Centerport had a few small fires but the biggest in town involved a mansion in Lloyd Harbor. Over a dozen Departments assisted The Huntington Fire Department; the lack of fire hydrants severely hindered the fire fighting capabilities. Other notables include Ex- Chiefs Ken Klerk and Earl Sammis celebreated 50 years of service, member Peter Reilly turning 90, and the arrival of the new Heavy Rescue truck. We hope you have enjoyed this book, the remainder is a pictorial reviewing our 100th anniversary celebration.

Centerport in 1998

Fire Headquarters, Huntington Beach Sub-Station, Catholic Chuch, Congregatonal Church, Methodist Church

LADIES' AUXILIARY
CENTERPORT FIRE DEPARTMENT

All wives and mothers of active and exempt firemen were invited to attend a meeting on February 13, 1940, 8 PM to discuss the organization of a Ladies' Auxiliary. Twenty-five women attended and, as they say, the rest is history. The Auxiliary was formally begun in March. The women instituted a Charter, enacted a Constitution and By-Laws, formulated committees and held elections.

According to the Auxiliary's constitution, "The purpose of the organization shall be to aid or assist the Centerport Fire Department in any way possible, to parade as a unit in any parades mandatory to the men of the Centerport Fire Department and to promote good will in the community.

The following women were the 39 original Charter Members:

Marion Benjamin	Teresa Boeckmann	Carolina Bohaty
Dorothea Braun	Patti Ferrer	Marie Graulich
May Heinicke	Marjorie Jones	Bessie Kellogg
Elsie Kohler	Katherine Kohler	Clara Lawson
Louise Lee	Marjorie Leonhardt	Florence L'Hommedieu
Anna Linck	Elsie Miller	Mary Moll
Gertrude Moran	Anna Morris	Dorothea Muckian
Alice Nichols	Emeline Nichols	Rose Patiky
Willa Reb	Mary Scudder	Ann Simpson
Frances Simpson	Lena Smith	Adeline Soper
Marion Soper	Matilda Soper	Catherine Stanka
Ann Stukalo	Susan Suydam	Helen Swan
Eva Utter	Betty Viafora	Kathryn Ward

Since its inception in 1940, there have been approximately 191 members admitted to the ranks of the Ladies' Auxiliary, which includes the original charter members.

Presently the following ladies are members of the Auxiliary:

Winnie Bohaty, Chaplain	Alice Jennings
Andrea Cunningham, President	Ann Knoph
Joan Feeley, Treas.	Nancy Knoph
Linda Grundas	Leigh Ann Varese, V.P.
Michele Hudson, Sec.	

Throughout their 60 years history, the auxiliary has been active in fundraising and has donated proceeds to various local organizations. They have assisted the department at fairs, tournaments and have been called on to serve hot coffee and refreshments day or night after large fires, often with their children in tow. Whether membership was high or low, the women have marched in parades, manned ticket booths, hosted Halloween and New Year's Eve parties, Christmas parties for the children and held an annual picture night. They've hosted luncheons, put on fashion shows and invited neighboring Auxiliaries to "coffee klatch".

The ladies of the Auxiliary are dedicated to their organization, their goals and the firefighters who are their husbands and children. There will always be a group of committed women to help out when necessary as long as there is a Centerport Fire Department.

LADIES' AUXILIARY PRAYER

The ladies wait, while their men respond,
united as one in a common bond.
The bond of serving, each in their own way,
the needs that arise, be what they may.
The reheated meals, the unsipped drink,
are a common occurrence, much more than you think.
It's mostly routine and done without flair,
the men return, their ladies are there.
But then comes the call, the tough one to fight,
a working fire that may last through the night.
The ladies again wait, but this time they know,
that sooner or later, they too will go.
As they wait for the signal, the time draws near,
for that sooner or later to be suddenly here.
The men are all weary, some of them spent,
the refreshments that arrive are like heaven sent.
The auxiliary, in fact, is more than a name.
It's a dedicated arm of the volunteer game.
So God when we pray for the firemen's care,
include the ladies, who were also there.

Joan Feeley, Auxiliary Treasurer

Families in the Centerport Fire Department

Families in the Centerport Fire Department

At any hour
That call may come
No matter when or who
or even where
The silent heroes emerge to keep us safe.

The distant wail of the siren
echoing off the harbor
in the dark of night
when all was quiet;
A subtle reminder that they risk their lives for ours.

A century of caring
Volunteers in the truest sense of the word
may their humanity and
selflessness flourish for years to come.

C.A.S.

Centerport in 1998

Post Office, Centerport Harbor, Little Neck Stores, Vanderbilt Museum
Tung-Ting, Centerport harbor, The "Shack", Little Neck & 25A

Eagle Truck Company #1

Engine Company #1

Engine Company #2

Fire Police

Rescue Squad

Scuba Squad

Ladies Auxillary

Cadets

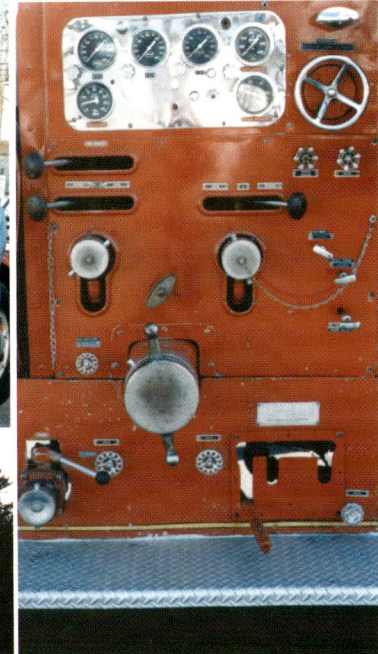

1944 Mack
Before
Restoration

During Restoration

The Restoration
took years to return the
1944 Mack to its original
condition.

Photos Courtesy of Jim Feeley

The Installation of the
1998 Officers at
the 100th Anniversary
Installation Dinner

Memorial Day 1998

Even though it rained on our parade that didn't stop us.

The un-veiling of the first of three commemorative stones.

A boat trip on a beautiful summers night on Long Island Sound

CENTERPORT FIRE DEPARTMENT
CENTENNIAL
1898-1998
CENTERPORT, LONG ISLAND

The Summer Cookout
at Camp Alvernia

The Kids had their day too!

Our Parade
down 25A to the
Firehouse

Muster and Fireworks at Centerport Beach

100th Anniversary
Memorial Service
held at the Firehouse
in honor of the original
members of C.F.D.

Holiday Cheer

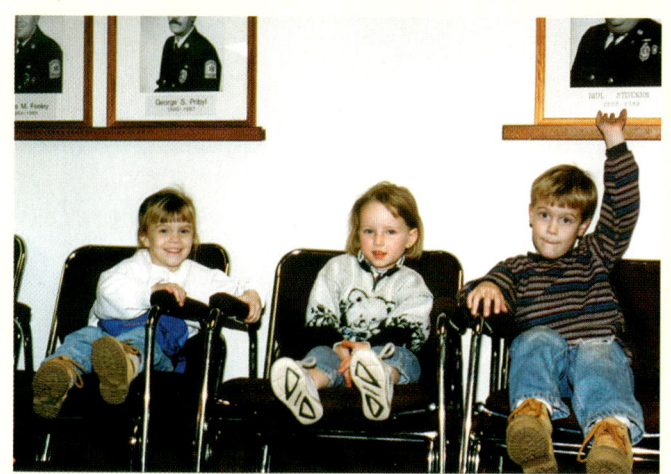

Congratulations Earl Sammis & Ken Klerk on 50 years active Service!!!

100th Anniversary Book Committee

Chairman
Jack W. Geffken, D.O.

Editor
Casey Doughtery

Writers

Kevin Gallagher

Deborah Geffken

John Giacoppi

Erin Reilly

Layout

Harry Burr

Jack Geffken

John Giacoppi

Computer Scanning

Jack Geffken

Data Entry
Joan Feeley

Research

Harry Burr

Douglas Davidson

Kevin Gallagher

Jack Geffken

Paul Heglund

Sam Jones

Karl Marusak

Lou Rispoli

Earl Sammis

William Wamp Jr.

Gus Zeis

Conrad Zinc

Special thanks to: The Huntington Historical Society, The Greenlawn-Centerport Historical Society, The Vanderbilt Museum, Camp Alvernia, Steve Silverman our Department Photographer, Chuck Belensky our Past Photographer, Bill Syracuse our Past Historian, & Mrs. Harvey Weber

Corporate Sponsors of
The Centerport Fire Department Anniversary Book

Bottles & Cases   143 Main Street Huntington   423-WINE

Advanced Lighting Corporation   30 Raynor Ave.   Ronkonkoma   467-4877

Your "Buds" at Clare Rose   72 Clare Rose Blvd.   Patchogue

Greenlawn Hardware   83 Broadway   Greenlawn   261-0119

Brentwood Fire Department

Greenlawn Fire Department - Columbia Hook & Ladder

Centereach Fire Department

Classic Golf Inc - Customized Greens & Tees   262-8953

Friends of The Centerport Fire Department

Andrew & Yveline Schroeder	Cotswold Drive	Centerport	N.Y.
William Wechter	Washington Drive	Centerport	N.Y.
Marie Censoplano	Sea Spray Drive	Centerport	N.Y.
Otto & Rosemary Franke	Midwood Drive	Centerport	N.Y.
Phyllis Cornell	Little Neck Road	Centerport	N.Y.
Peter & Helen Pastorelli	Little Neck Road	Centerport	N.Y.
William & Kathleen Tschinkel	Taft Crescent	Centerport	N.Y.
Paul & Gladys Schoenberg	Little Neck Road	Centerport	N.Y.
Kenneth & Dianne Klarman	Makanna Drive	Centerport	N.Y.
Stephen Mc Mahon	Meade Drive	Centerport	N.Y.
Harry Graw	Truman Place	Centerport	N.Y.
Centerport Homemakers Unit	Park Circle	Centerport	N.Y.
George & Sharon Byrd	Hayes Place	Centerport	N.Y.
Bernard & Eithne Cleary	Taylor Street	Centerport	N.Y.
Patrick & Elizabeth Madigan	Adams Street	Centerport	N.Y.
Melvin & Risa Leeds	Fleets Cove Road	Huntington	N.Y.
Alfred Baker	Jackson Crescent	Centerport	N.Y.
Raymond & Helen Gargan	Fillmore Street	Centerport	N.Y.
John & Madeline Kane	Salem Ridge Drive	Huntington	N.Y.
Virginia Schissel	Salem Ridge Drive	Huntington	N.Y.
Melvin Schmidt	Fleets Cove Road	Huntington	N.Y.
John & Barbara Cavanagh	P.O. Box 224	Centerport	N.Y.
James & Margaret De Santis	Cranbrook Drive	Centerport	N.Y.
Stephen & Mary Sumakis	Renwick Avenue	Huntington	N.Y.
Mr. & Mrs. Mario Valesio	Idle Day Drive	Centerport	N.Y.
Michael & Nancy Montelli	Loneoak Court	Centerport	N.Y.
Joseph & Grace Saladino	Little Bull Court	Centerport	N.Y.
Frank & Mary Kaestner	P.O. Box 498	Centerport	N.Y.
Robert & Christina Dolce	Fillmore Street	Centerport	N.Y.
Douglas & Eileen Hunt	Quay Court	Centerport	N.Y.
Douglas & Margaret Davidson	Jefferson Street	Centerport	N.Y.
Joseph & Nina Doherty	Topsfield Lane	Huntington	N.Y.
Thomas & Frances Pirro	Makanna Drive	Huntington	N.Y.
Andrew & Carol Longo	Prospect Road	Centerport	N.Y.
Norbert & Jane Hansen	Harbor Park Drive	Centerport	N.Y.
Doug & Jennifer Haluza	Johnson Street	Centerport	N.Y.
Margaret Connors	Jackson Crescent	Centerport	N.Y.
Thomas & BettyAnn Travers	Oakdale Drive	Centerport	N.Y.
Ronald Carman, C.P.A.	Hawthorne Court	Centerport	N.Y.
Diane Ingerson & Robert Brancaccio	Ridge Field Drive	Centerport	N.Y.
James & Gail Welsch	Connelly Road	Huntington	N.Y.
William & Marieanne Wason	Little Neck Road	Centerport	N.Y.
Stanley & Marilyn Koven	P.O. Box 630	Centerport	N.Y.
Douglas Esposit	Centershore Road	Centerport	N.Y.
Raymond & Margaret Russell	Harbor Park Drive	Centerport	N.Y.
Paricia Grady	Hoover Place	Centerport	N.Y.
Iadanza & Schultz C.P.A's	Centerport Road	Centerport	N.Y.
William & Linda Kirkpatrick	Little Neck Road	Centerport	N.Y.
Edward & Judith Kamykowski	Wainer Court	Centerport	N.Y.
The Consorte Family	Harbor Circle	Centerport	N.Y.
Richard & Dale Johanson	Harbor Circle	Centerport	N.Y.
Vincent & Bessie Panettieri	Mallard Cove	Centerport	N.Y.
Kenneth & Helena Kuhn	Bankside Drive	Centerport	N.Y.
Anne Crandell	Mohawk Street	Centerport	N.Y.

Friends of The Centerport Fire Department

Clarence & Jeannette Kopp	P.O. Box 493	Centerport	N.Y.
Charles & Lauren Trifiro	Little Neck Road	Centerport	N.Y.
Margaret Blakley	Arthur Street	Centerport	N.Y.
Barabra Yates	Sherry Court	Centerport	N.Y.
Ralph & Florence Byrnes	Harbor Park Court	Centerport	N.Y.
Vincent & Rose Marie Morando	Cranbrook Drive	Centerport	N.Y.
James & Helen Kelly	Waterview Drive	Centerport	N.Y.
The Averbuch Family	Laurel Hill Road	Centerport	N.Y.
Dominick Netti	McKinley Terrace	Centerport	N.Y.
Lawrence & Barabara Betz	Mariners Court	Centerport	N.Y.
Ellen & Sam Jaffee	Adams Street	Centerport	N.Y.
Mr. & Mrs. Micheal Ianelli	Spring Hollow Road	Centerport	N.Y.
Richard & Louise Climo	Truman Place	Centerport	N.Y.
Tom & Ruth Rost	Mariners Court	Centerport	N.Y.
John & Eleanor Favre	P.O.Box 367	Centerport	N.Y.
Russell & Laura Sapienza	Salem Ridge Drive	Huntington	N.Y.
Irene Neff	Little Neck Road	Centerport	N.Y.
Ed & Betty Gates & Family	Little Bull Court	Centerport	N.Y.
Stephen & Diane Lahood	Mariners Court	Centerport	N.Y.
Paul & Donatella Mazzarella	Ridgeview Lane	Huntington	N.Y.
Sheila Hubbs	Coolidge Drive	Centerport	N.Y.
Joyce & John Roth	Washington Drive	Centerport	N.Y.
The Geluso & Hannemann Families	Merriwood Court	Huntington	N.Y.
John & Yvonne O'Connor	Merriwood Court	Huntington	N.Y.
Geoffrey Gardner	Little Neck Road	Centerport	N.Y.
John & Irene Donovan	Laurel Hill Road	Centerport	N.Y.
Thomas & Kathleen Shea	Makanna Drive	Huntington	N.Y.
Peter & Jennifer Shore	Harbor Park Drive	Centerport	N.Y.
John & Kathleen Lawlor	Van Buren Drive	Centerport	N.Y.
Allen & Carole Rubenstein	Washington Drive	Centerport	N.Y.
Joseph & Mary Ann Rondone	Forest Drive	Centerport	N.Y.
Peter Saros	Taft Crescent	Centerport	N.Y.
Raymond & Margaret Fassberger	Mill Dam Road	Centerport	N.Y.
Jean Agresta	Ridgeview Lane	Centerport	N.Y.
Edmee & Harald Hubscher	Little Neck Road	Centerport	N.Y.
Dr. Joshua & Jerene Weitman	Harned Drive	Centerport	N.Y.
Paul & Mary Mariani	Johnson Street	Centerport	N.Y.
Lawrence & Carol Anne Richards	Harbor Park Court	Centerport	N.Y.
Ellen Schoenberg	Coolidge Street	Centerport	N.Y.
Paul & Judy Hoertz	Oneonta Court	Centerport	N.Y.
Michael & Leigh Sterflinger	Westbrook Court	Greenlawn	N.Y.
William & Geraldine Baker	Westbrook Court	Greenlawn	N.Y.
Scott & Mary Jo Friedman	Buchanan Street	Centerport	N.Y.
Kalman Bergen	Idle Day Drive	Centerport	N.Y.
Donald & Catherine Broggini	Idle Day Knoll	Centerport	N.Y.
Pierre & Anne Hulsart	Van Buren Drive	Centerport	N.Y.
Edward & Dolores Basso	Mill Dam Road	Centerport	N.Y.
Genevieve Baron	Greenhaven Way	Centerport	N.Y.
Eugene & Linda Lehnert	North Drive	Centerport	N.Y.
Charles & Margaret Jordan	Washington Drive	Centerport	N.Y.
Gerald & Shirley Levy	Cherry Lane	Huntington	N.Y.
Robert & Helen Grenke	Cherry Lane	Huntington	N.Y.
Norbert Nardone	Stony Hollow Road	Centerport	N.Y.

Friends of The Centerport Fire Department

Linda Fromia	Lone Oak Drive	Centerport	N.Y.
Norma Ehrlich	Harbor Park Court	Centerport	N.Y.
Anne Lepore	Clevland Drive	Centerport	N.Y.
Todd Davis & Audrey Venezia	Judy Court	Centerport	N.Y.
Margaret & Douglas Davidson	Jefferson Street	Centerport	N.Y.
Paul & Barbara Esatto	Harbor Circle	Centerport	N.Y.
Albert & Karen Messineo	Maryanne Court	Huntington	N.Y.
Mary Frances Weiss	Garfield Street	Centerport	N.Y.
Scott, Susan, & Kristin Moran		Centerport	N.Y.
Edward & Kathleen Gradel	Tuscarora Drive	Centerport	N.Y.
Johanna Eleanore & Adloph Aebisher	Old Northport Road	Huntington	N.Y.
Robert & Mary White	Mayflower Court	Centerport	N.Y.
Andrew & Maryann Mank	Quay Court	Centerport	N.Y.
Gloria Nass	Van Buren Drive	Centerport	N.Y.
The Forstbauer Family	Coolidge Drive	Centerport	N.Y.
George & Rita Rohloff	Harbor Ridge Drive	Centerport	N.Y.
Albert & Alice Rosanes	Paul Revere Lane	Centerport	N.Y.
Russell & Alice Brooks	Westfield Drive	Centerport	N.Y.
Michael & Louise Kelly	Monroe Drive	Centerport	N.Y.
Robert & Patricia McAlpine	Little Neck Road	Centerport	N.Y.
Mark Zambratto Consulting	Spring Hollow Road	Centerport	N.Y.
Felicia Kelsey	Washington Drive	Centerport	N.Y.
Morton Smith, Jr.	Laurel Hill Road	Centerport	N.Y.
W.J. Bradford, Jr.	Harbor Ridge Drive	Centerport	N.Y.
Joseph & Beatrice Carillo	Little Neck Road	Centerport	N.Y.
Paul & Stephanie Sadagursky	Hawthorne Court	Centerport	N.Y.
Hand Surgery Associates of L.I.	E. Main Street	Huntington	N.Y.
George & Isabelle Pullis	Benham Court	Centerport	N.Y.
Patrick & Maryann Gilmartin	Upper Pond Court	Centerport	N.Y.
Frederick & Marjorie Losen	Gina Drive	Centerport	N.Y.
Viola Maher	Keith Court	Centerport	N.Y.
Karl & Connie Ritter	McKinley Terrace	Centerport	N.Y.
Morton & Norma Ehrlich	Harbor Park Court	Centerport	N.Y.
Frank &Mary Kaestner	P.O. Box 498	Centerport	N.Y.
Fritzi Gros-Daillon	Paul Revere Lane	Centerport	N.Y.
Frank & Carol Ann Fischer	Sherry Court	Centerport	N.Y.
Ralph Byrnes	Harbor Park Court	Centerport	N.Y.
Donna Courdoff-Bemiss & Robert Bemiss	Oakwood Road	Huntington	N.Y.
John & Barbara Lee Cavanagh	Mill Dam Road	Centerport	N.Y.
Roger & Margaret Kohl	Ridgefield Road	Centerport	N.Y.
Centerport Delicatessen	Little Neck Road	Centerport	N.Y.
Robert & Andrea Maire	Little Neck Road	Centerport	N.Y.
Belle & Julius Gorkin	Ridgeview Lane	Huntington	N.Y.
Violet Bradney	Stony Hollow Road	Centerport	N.Y.
Kristin & Joseph Pangia	Harrison Drive	Centerport	N.Y.
Frank & Brigid Pavlik	Centerport Road	Centerport	N.Y.
Frank Alfano	Mill Dam Road	Centerport	N.Y.
Thomas & Janet Antorino	Washington Drive	Centerport	N.Y.
Philip & Gloria Clegg	Beach Plum Drive	Centerport	N.Y.
Lorraine Moranville	Tuscarora Drive	Centerport	N.Y.
Michael & Patricia Doherty	Idle Day Drive	Centerport	N.Y.
Bernie & Oran Perks	Prospect Road	Centerport	N.Y.
George & Frances Olsen	E. Main Street	Centerport	N.Y.
Fred Juliano	Oakdale Drive	Centerport	N.Y.

Friends of The Centerport Fire Department

The Nicolette Family	Spring Hollow Road	Centerport	N.Y.
Donald & Wima Walker	Coolidge Drive	Centerport	N.Y.
Celeste Morin	Prospect Road	Centerport	N.Y.
J&J Vavrina	Centershore Road	Centerport	N.Y.
The Malico Family	Washington Drive	Centerport	N.Y.
Anton Polacek	Shawnee Street	Centerport	N.Y.
Borg & Borg Insurance	East Main Street	Huntington	N.Y.
Mahan Construction	Prospect Road	Centerport	N.Y.
Christopher & Anne Long	Johnson Street	Centerport	N.Y.
Helen Kucera	P.O. Box 405	Centerport	N.Y.
Natalie Perrine	Spring Hollow Road	Centerport	N.Y.
Marion Feeley	Fleets Cove Road	Huntington	N.Y.
Richard & Leslie Tarkin	Bankside Drive	Centerport	N.Y.
Jose Lopez	Little Neck Road	Centerport	N.Y.
Anna Soule	Mohawk Street	Centerport	N.Y.
Russel &Alice Artzt	Rolling Hill Lane	Old Westbury	N.Y.
Ann & Bryan Coakley	Oakdale Road	Centerport	N.Y.
Margaret Corcoran Dempsey	Tuscarora Drive	Centerport	N.Y.
Edward & Pauline Fischel	Little Neck Road	Centerport	N.Y.
Phyllis Cornell	Little Neck Road	Centerport	N.Y.

Bibliography

Carruth, Gordon, *The Encyclopedia of American facts and Dates,* 10th Edition, HarperCollins, New York, 1997

Smith, Dennis, *Dennis Smith's History of Firefighting in America: 300 Years of Courage,* Dial Press, New York, 1978

Weber, Harvey, *Centerport,* HB Davis, New York,1990

Centerport Fire Department Archives, Minutes of the Department Meetings: 1888 – 1998

Centerport Fire District Archives, Minutes of the District Meetings: 1924 – 1998

Historical Documents from: Huntington Historical Society, Greenlawn – Centerport Historical Society, Vanderbilt Museum, Camp Alvernia

News Clippings: *Newsday; The Long Islander; The Brooklyn Eagle*

Various Public Internet Sites